Loving Your Man Without Losing Your Mind

Susie Davis

Regal

From Gospel Light
Ventura, California, U.S.A.

Published by Regal Books
From Gospel Light
Ventura, California, U.S.A.

Library of Congress Cataloging-in-Publication Data
Davis, Susie, 1963-
Loving your man without losing your mind / Susie Davis.
    p. cm.
ISBN 978-0-8307-4371-1 (trade paper)
    1. Marriage—Religious aspects—Christianity. 2. Man-woman relationships—Religious
aspects—Christianity. 3. Wives—Religious life. I. Title.
BV835.D385 2007
248.8'435—dc22
                                                                                    2007001924

1 2 3 4 5 6 7 8 9 10 / 10 09 08 07

Rights for publishing this book in other languages are contracted by Gospel Light
Worldwide, the international nonprofit ministry of Gospel Light. For additional information, visit www.gospellightworldwide.org.

To Will, the man of my dreams and the love of my life.

*I will give them a heart to know Me, for I am the L*ORD.

JEREMIAH 24:7, *NASB*

Contents

Section One: Crash Course on Couple's Communication

Section Two: The Garden of Disenchantment

Section Three: Fatal Detraction

Section Four: Friendly Fire

A C K N O W L E D G M E N T S

Thanks to . . .

My fabulous family: Will, Will III, Emily and Sara. You are my real wealth, my greatest joy on Earth!

My parents: Peg and Bob Gerrie, for modeling love and devotion in marriage for 50 years.

My in-laws: Ann and Will Davis, for modeling love and devotion in marriage for 52 years.

My e-Group: Jodi Allen, Liz Benigno, Diahn (Dee) Ehlers and Julie Washington, for reading and responding with wisdom and truth.

My wonderful literary agent: Bill Jensen.

My "last-minute" editor: Terri Crow.

My friend, ministry partner and publicist: Andrea Smith.

And finally, a big thanks to my publishing family at Regal, and especially to Alex Field for being such an amazing encourager.

e-Group Explained

When I first started writing this book, the process was full steam ahead, but it didn't take me more than a few chapters to realize that I needed input from other married women. So I prayed and asked God for direction about seeking readers to review my newly written chapters. I wanted to make sure I was hitting the truth about marriage. I desired authentic feedback about how I was handling the subjects. I wanted the opinions of others on various marital issues. And another thing I realized: I didn't want to do ministry alone.

So I started off by emailing a few married friends who I knew would be gut-level honest with me. I explained the situation and asked if they would be willing to read each chapter as I finished it and then test the material on their own marriages. Four women agreed to the proposal. Since they played such a huge role in shaping this resource, let me introduce them to you now.

Meet my friend Dee. She's not only the hard-core editor of the group, but she's also a fabulous riding instructor. For 10 years, she trained me in all things pertaining to riding and care of horses (riding is one of my favorite hobbies). Dee has been married to Blake for 20 years.

Then there's Jodi. She is the tender heart in the e-Group. Her compassion for people is such an example to me. And she's really funny in a quiet, surprising way. She has been married to Erick for 16 years.

Julie is our newlywed in the group. She and David have been married six fabulously blissful months. And to those of you who've been married for a while who might think she won't have much to say to you—watch out. Some of her comments rocked my world.

Then there's Liz. She is a tenacious woman of faith. Her thoughts on marriage are so real and raw you might just feel like hugging her through the page. She and her husband, Steve, have been married 18 years.

With my e-Group assembled, we started a process that looked something like this: I would write a chapter, then I would send it to them, and over the next week their comments would trickle back to me via email. Well, right away I noticed something really amazing. When my friends emailed their comments and insights, they not only improved my chapters but also enriched my marriage. Over the course of six months, while writing this book, the interaction with my friends served a vital role in encouraging my devotion to my husband, Will. As I discovered how they felt about important issues, I was challenged to think deeply about the issues too. As we continued that weekly communication, some incredibly important truths were exchanged online.

But there was another blessing that surprised and deeply pleased me. In the process of including these friends in my ministry effort, I discovered a little community of godly women—my circle of encouragers, who nurtured my faith and my marriage. My interaction with them reminded me that no matter how busy my days may seem, I desperately need other women in my life. I need them because they play a part in strengthening my spiritual life. Their perspectives help me to be a better wife and mother. And most important, their presence has helped me to be a better God-lover.

This small group has provided me with such insight that I just couldn't imagine keeping the wisdom from you. So I have done something unique in this book: I've allowed you to see their responses at the end of the chapters. After the section of study questions, you'll find a section called *e-Group*—which is my abbreviation of *Encourager Group*. In the *e-Group* section, you'll find responses from Dee, Jodi, Julie and Liz. No doubt they will encourage you and offer a different outlook from mine. I'm sure you will enjoy their enlightening, funny and often touching words.

But more than that, I would love for you to find a group of encouragers for your life and marriage. Paul tells us, "When we get together, I want to encourage you in your faith, but I also want to be encouraged by yours" (see Rom. 1:12). We all need to prompt each other in faithfulness to God and our husbands. I encourage you to take this book and get together with a friend. Start a book club or a neighborhood Bible study, or make a weekly coffee date with a few friends. Or if you're like me and close to a computer all day, you can even form a group via email. But whatever you do, start an e-Group. Get in contact with a few people who are interested in strengthening their marriage, read a chapter a week and talk about it! Listen to each other, encourage one another and pray, pray, pray for your marriages. I promise you'll get far more out of your discussions than you can imagine. And you might find, just like I did, that the meeting together and sharing will change your life and your marriage for the better.

Loving Your Man Without Losing Your Mind

I don't recall exactly what we were talking about that Saturday morning. For that matter, neither does my husband, Will, but both of us definitely remember the *exact* words I said at the end of the "disagreement."

I looked at him across the kitchen table and said in all seriousness, "I think Satan is attacking our marriage."

"Why?" he responded quizzically.

"Because," I stated emphatically, *"you are driving me crazy!"*

Will tilted his head back and laughed . . . but I didn't. I meant it. I felt he was pushing me to the utter limits of reason and marital civility. This man I love and have committed to live with forever was in the process of *driving me absolutely insane!*

If you have been married for even a short while, no doubt you can relate. And so here are the questions: What is it about marriage that seems to push us to the point of breaking? Why is marriage so much harder than anyone ever dared to imagine? And how could the one man that a woman loves *most* in the world end up becoming the one person she struggles to live in harmony with?

Many couples divorce because they've been pushed past the point of breaking, but ask any young bride just starting out if she wants a happy marriage and of course she'll say yes. For the majority of women, a happy marriage is the dream of a lifetime.

And yet, how many marriages stall out in a "catatonic covenant"—doomed by relational wreckage because even trying to get along sends them into crazy land? You know, a lifetime of *just getting by* until "death do us part." Kind of like some bizarre, silent agreement to hang on in torment "for as long as you both shall live." This is not what little girls dream of when thinking of the one human relationship meant to fulfill the deepest longing of their hearts. Rather, a little girl grows into a woman with hopes of being loved and adored. She longs for an unconditional, loving relationship with her husband. A relationship built to stand strong in the inevitable storms of life, with a promise of more satisfying love waiting on the other side.

But for many, it seems as though these dreams leave us destitute on the altar of life, longing for more. As marriages fall apart and divorce rates climb, it would appear the dream is just that—a dream. Can a happy marriage be a reality in today's society? And if so, how can couples accomplish this worthwhile goal?

The truth is, both husbands and wives know the reality: Marriage is the hardest thing they have ever undertaken, requiring far more energy, investment and work to survive (much less succeed) than they ever imagined. And while it takes two to tango, this book is for the wives out there—for wives who realize that marriage takes effort. For wives who realize that marriage is complex and critical. Demanding and deserving. Exhausting and exhilarating. For wives who understand that marriage is worth the attention of a lifetime. And for wives willing to admit that there have been times in marriage when the very thing that has best communicated their true feelings about their husband is the phrase: "You're driving me crazy!"

A woman needs to understand how to deal with the man she loves. She needs support to live with her spouse in a godly way. She needs to know that just because her man might be driving her crazy, that doesn't mean she can't count on God to give her the marriage of her dreams. She needs perspective and truth, along with some practical help.

In *Loving Your Man Without Losing Your Mind*, you can expect to encounter a biblical perspective on marriage. Expect practical tips intended to open the door to loving your man with an abundance of understanding and grace. In addition, expect God to exceed your own expectations for a happy marriage—with His help, you can have the marriage of a lifetime, the "happily ever after" kind!

This book will explore all the "biggies" where conflict and problems in marriage are concerned. *Loving Your Man Without Losing Your Mind* is designed to offer straight talk, encouragement, laughter and hope for loving the man of your dreams—your husband. No more *monotonous monogamy*! Instead, unlock the secrets to loving your man with your whole heart and your whole mind—"in holy matrimony, for as long as you both shall live." Amen!

Crash Course on Couple's Communication

I recently got a speeding ticket. So instead of letting my mistake ruin my driving record and raise insurance rates, I decided to take a defensive driving course (with two teenaged drivers, we need all the help we can get in our family). Now, because I detest sitting in windowless rooms for hours on end, listening to instructors drone on and on about the correct usage of turn signals and the like, I looked for an online class. I figure that sitting in my own home, listening to a computerized voice drone on and on is much easier to swallow. After paying for the course, I logged on—and was struck that the reason I disliked this online class so much, even before I started, was that *I already knew how to drive.* Still, with a roll of my eyes and a deep sigh, I settled in to catch the information necessary to pass the test at the end of the six-hour course.

It's possible that when you read this section title, you had a reaction similar to mine when I logged on for that driving course. In fact, you might even be tempted to skip over this marriage material because *you already know how to communicate.* And it's true. You do already know how to communicate with your husband, but there's a chance you're just like me—you've made mistakes and you need a refresher course. Maybe, just maybe, you've been speeding carelessly along in your communication with your spouse.

What I found in my defensive driving class is that as much as I didn't want to take the course, I learned a lot—it made me a better driver. The material presented in this section will make you a better wife. The time you spend reading these four chapters will remind you of the importance of words and attitudes. Being able to communicate effectively in marriage is critical because it's often a safeguard against a costly, perhaps deadly, relational wreck. So get really comfortable—I promise not to drone on and on—and let's look into the facts about men and women when it comes to marriage communication.

CHAPTER 1

Love in Translation

Why What You Say and How You Treat
Your Husband Really Matter

Men don't ask for directions while driving. Wise women know this, and they remember it when they are tempted to push, prod or beg a man to stop and ask another man—say a gas station attendant—for assistance. Most smart women understand that it's a real sign of maleness for a guy to figure out where he is in any city in America without help from anyone else—especially a woman. This is a rule I have been aware of for at least 20 years . . . because I have been married 20 years. But it is a rule I chose to ignore when my husband, Will, and I were lost in Orange County last summer.

Will and I were in California taping a DVD curriculum piece on marriage. The trip was quick, just three days, and the only prayer I uttered day after day before we left was that we would not argue. Because of my experience as a drama teacher, I knew that you really couldn't fake liking each other in front of a camera with all those unconscious nonverbal things going on. And I knew, just knew, deep down in my bones that if Will and I were in a funk, everyone viewing the marriage DVD would be able to tell. So my prayer was that God would help us to really love and enjoy each other as we completed the seven-hour taping session.

It was a long but fun process, and God did answer my prayers—there was no funky weirdness between the two of us at all while taping. Whew. But with all the prayers answered and all the taping behind us, I somehow lapsed into a state of exhaustion and stupidity as we were driving back to the hotel late that last night. My eyes roamed the darkened landscape as we drove along, and I noticed that we were traveling in places that looked unfamiliar. Without thinking, I blurted out, "Will, I don't remember coming in this way—I think we're lost!"

"Yes," Will replied. "I might have missed a turn, but we're not far off at all."

I immediately straightened up in my seat and went for the printed driving instructions. Suddenly I had plenty of energy and even persuaded Will to stop for gas while I bolted inside to ask the attendant for confirmation that we were headed in the right direction. This was not a good idea, of course—I was violating every piece of wisdom I knew about men in general and about my man in particular. Long story short, Will quickly corrected the directional mistake and headed in the right direction, while I quickly created fertile ground for an argument, thereby heading in the wrong direction. Not too smart on my part. I transformed a missed turn into, well, marital mayhem.

Where's a Map for the Maze?

The drive back to the hotel was still and quiet. I imagine Will was ruminating over my impetuous actions, and I was starting to realize that my impatience had created a "situation." Then suddenly, as if out of nowhere, all the words started tumbling out. He would say something and I would respond. I would say something and he would retort. Word upon word played out without one winning hand. When we finally got to the hotel, we dragged our tired bodies (and mouths) to the room and crawled into bed feeling defeated, discouraged and without any desire to make things better.

The courses of true love never did run smooth.

—William Shakespeare

What happened that evening in California was not a singular event in the Davis marriage—not getting lost physically on a darkened roadway but getting lost in a maze of marital miscommunication. Sometimes it just happens. It isn't that we don't love each other—it's just that those communication ditches open up and we tumble into them.

In the instance I just recounted, it wasn't so much that I was trying to annoy and anger Will—it was more that I just wasn't really thinking . . . at all. I blurted out what I thought, without considering how my words would impact Will and the rest of the evening. I started talking, acting on the immediacy of the situation, and accelerated from 0 to 60 in a matter of seconds—words spilling out furiously, consideration for my husband totally absent. I wasn't talking *with* Will as much as I was talking *at* Will, if you know what I mean. I was floating around in the Sea of Me and letting my words toss and turn in any which way without regard for Will. And that lapse in judgment just happened to land us in a fight. Things might have turned out differently if I had been thinking more clearly or if Will had had a longer fuse, but on that particular night, the circumstances were just right for an argument. Sometimes it happens . . . yes, even to a ministry couple.

I tell you this because I want you to know straight up that my marriage isn't perfect (and actually, that is not at all what I am after—I don't even know what a "perfect marriage" looks like). But I can tell you what I am after in my marriage: I desire to be married to Will until I die—that is my dream. And I want to love him, truly love him. And I want to be a woman he can love in return.

Why We Act Worst with the One We Love Most

In real life, this is where things can get a bit tricky, because what I do and what I say are not always an accurate reflection of how I really feel. My words and actions often mirror the fluctuating upheavals of daily living—instead of manifesting how much I love Will. Maybe you understand what I'm talking about. You love your husband, really love him, but as true as your love is, it doesn't always show. Instead of reciting "how do I love thee, let me count the ways," you recite for your husband a litany of the irritations of the day. The trivial stuff like getting lost in the car. Or fussing over a bill. Or a disagreement about how to handle one of the kids. Just the everyday stuff that wears you down. And while that everyday stuff is just a part of life, the problem is that everyday bickering rips into the heart of your marital relationship. It creates tension. And though you desire to be a loving wife, you know the day-to-day "stuff" often stands in the way.

I have struggled with this very issue. I call it the "love most, act worst" philosophy. The people I absolutely love the most—my husband and my kids—often get the worst of me. The everyday frustrations often shred me to pieces, and I end up giving little tiny bits of goodness to my family instead of the huge chunks they deserve.

We flatter those we scarcely know
We please the fleeting guest
And deal full many a thoughtless blow
To those who love us best.
—Ella Wheeler Wilcox

As badly as I feel about this, I know I'm not alone in practicing this philosophy. So if any of this sounds familiar, imagine right now what would happen if a member of your family were seriously hurt in an accident. It would create a kind of singular clarity in your life. You would drop everything, realizing the importance of the person's life, and concentrate on communicating how you really feel. Your words and your actions would reflect your priorities in a real way. Your love would be openly manifested. No fighting. No snippy ugly words. No verbal or nonverbal communication that reflects anything other than how you desperately love the person, irritations aside. You would be operating on the "love most, act best" philosophy instead of the "love most, act worst" philosophy.

"Love most, act best" living creates peace in life. It produces joy in life. And it gives you the satisfaction of living a life that is in line with your real priorities. It means that you communicate through your actions and your words a deeply felt affection for the people you love.

Translating the Truth

Recently I was reading a book that completely summed up my ongoing attempt to understand the irony of the "love most, act worst" philosophy. It was a paragraph buried in Dr. Emerson Emmerich's *Love and Respect*. He was expounding on a verse in Titus 2:4, which reads, "These older women must train the younger women to love their husbands and their children." The insight I'd been looking for came in understanding the translation of one little word: "love."

> Here older women are told to encourage younger women to love their husbands and children, but in this case, Paul is not talking about *agape* love. In Titus 2:4, he uses the Greek word *phileo*, which refers to the human, brotherly kind of love. The point is, a young wife is created to

agape her husband and children. Ultimately, she will never stop unconditionally loving them. But in the daily wear and tear of life, she is in danger of becoming discouraged—so discouraged that she may lack *phileo*. A kind of impatient unfriendliness can come over her. She may scold and sigh way too much. After all, there is always something or someone who needs correcting. She cares deeply. Her motives are filled with *agape*, but her methods lack *phileo*.[1]

When I read that, it was as if a light bulb popped on. It finally made sense to me why I could love Will with everything inside of me and still treat him like crud when he made a wrong turn in the car.

I need more *phileo* love for Will. And I need that *phileo* love because that is what will enable me to communicate my real affection for him. It is what will help me to hand out big chunks of goodness to my husband in the form of what I do and say. And it will help me to live out the "love most, act best" philosophy with more ease.

What about you? Do your words and actions betray your deep-down love for your husband? Is there some impatient unfriendliness floating around in your marriage? If so, chances are that there is something getting lost in translation. And do you know what is likely getting sidelined in all those moments? *The relationship.* Quarrelling is like an autoimmune disease, attacking at its core the very thing that a husband and wife cherish the most: their togetherness. Our petty quarrels have us acting like dummies on a crash course, wrecking the goodness of marriage.

I bet you don't want that in your marriage—and I don't either. What I really want is time well spent with Will. I want a marriage relationship of few regrets. I want to be a wife who is easy to love.

The only way I can be the woman I want to be is to lean into God and His way of doing things. It's what this book is about—about seeking God's guidance so that you can learn how to love the man you married and become the wife you really want to be, deep down inside. God made you and your husband. He is the One who can mold your marriage into all it needs to be.

And the great news? Considering how you communicate is a step in the right direction. You are one step closer to banning "the crazies" from your marriage. You are one step closer to loving your man without losing your mind! You are one step closer to loving with an irresistible affection and communicating with increasing kindness. So take a deep breath and know that today you are closer to your destination than you were yesterday. You can get to the place you both really want to be: side-by-side in that car together, enjoying the marriage of your dreams!

Loving Your Man

- What are the things/situations that create an impatient unfriendliness in your marriage?

- How often do you find yourself doing things that you know bother your husband? What would you say causes you to do those things?

- How would *phileo* love impact your daily interactions with your husband?

- While *phileo* love is a love characterized by fond affection, *agape* love is a love characterized by unconditional acceptance. Why is it important to have both types of love in your marriage?

• How do you give and receive *agape* love?

• How do you give and receive *phileo* love?

e-Group

This chapter made me cry. How can I have it all so backward? The concept of "love most, act worst" is lived out all the time in my home. After reading the chapter, I'm adjusting the way I see things. I'm trying to actually understand the way my family sees me. They don't always get the good stuff from me, but I certainly do dish that out to other people. Sure, my family has great moments together . . . but they are connected with hurried demands and terse words. Sometimes it's packaged in my skewed idea of being a productive wife and mother, and sometimes it's just because I'm tired and grouchy. And I know that neither is okay. In my everyday communication, I want my husband to understand how much I appreciate and admire him. And I want him to have the best of me, not the leftovers. The thought of handing out huge chunks of goodness to the ones who are precious to me sounds so satisfying. But the hard part is that I know it will take a lot of effort to change this pattern I've been living. Becoming a "love most, act best" wife and mother requires true desire and help from God. This chapter has changed the way I see myself, and I pray that it would haunt me every day until giving Erick and our kids the *really* good stuff just comes naturally.

—Jodi

Note
1. Emerson Eggerich, *Love and Respect* (Brentwood, TN: Integrity Publishers, 2004), p. 36.

CHAPTER 2

Fight Right

How to Fight Fair with Your Husband
Even When You Disagree

I love sitting on the front porch in my rocking chair first thing in the morning. There's just nothing more idyllic than gently rocking, steaming cup of coffee in hand, as I enjoy the morning sun streaming down. From where I sit, I can see the gentle curve of my sidewalk where the impatiens dip their bright pink faces over the walkway. I love listening to the birds sing and watching as my neighbors stroll by with their dogs.

It's so comforting—yet there is something I absolutely hate about it: the mosquitoes. They have taken over my neighborhood. Our friend Steve says the mosquitoes are so numerous that they could swoop in and carry a dog off—a really big dog—if only they were organized. Those stupid mosquitoes have wrecked many relaxing morning moments for me. I go out ready for beauty, only to end up continuously swatting the little pests as they swarm around me. Annoyed, I silently curse them as they bite my exposed skin and then I reluctantly spray myself down with insect repellent to keep them from drawing more blood. The first round of repellant spray doesn't do much to get rid of them, so I spray again 10 minutes later. And again in another 10. Despite my defensive ploys, these mosquitoes are vicious and aggressive, intent on wrecking my sweet spot in the morning. And they could be a deterrent to a serious mosquito hater like me, but I love the morning too much to let them stop me. So I spray away, realizing that it's the price I pay for enjoying the great outdoors.

The point of this story? Arguments are to relationships what bugs are to the great outdoors. The two don't exist without each other. If you go outside, expect some bugs. If you love someone, expect some conflict. The belief that "if you really love each other, you won't fight" is a lie that sets you up for relational disaster. Kind of like my sitting on my porch and expecting no mosquito bites—it just ain't gonna happen, honey. It's like wanting to enjoy the benefit of good communication without ever having to navigate the difficulties. Like expecting you'll get along with your spouse without ever working at it. The idea of conflict-free communication with your spouse is extremely unrealistic. So what's the answer? Find a healthy way to handle the conflicts.

Don't Let Conflict "Bug You Out"

If you've been married awhile, it's likely you've had your share of fights with your man. You've probably "discussed" things like the budget, chore distribution, in-laws and sex. These are all hot topics that seem to lead to communication turmoil. So let me just say right now—you're normal. Most American couples fight about those kinds of things. And while it's normal to fight, it's not always optimal for the relationship, right? If a fight turns into a heated screaming match that ends when you storm out of the room and slam the door, it can be devastating. Besides, treating your husband that way leaves you with a sick feeling in your stomach. After the smoke lifts, you feel alone and confused, wondering what to do. It's just not nice.

But there's hope. We just need to consult our guide to practical, godly living—the Bible. God's Word addresses these kinds of relational issues and is laden with great helps about how to get along with other people. The truth is that we're going to fight and have disagreements with our spouses, so we need to know how to fight in a way that honors God and our spouse.

Understanding Anger

First off, let's start with some basic biblical truth: The Bible does not condemn anger. In Psalm 4:4, it actually says, *"In your anger do not sin"* (*NIV*, emphasis added), so know this with all certainty: *It is not wrong for you or your husband to feel angry.* If you and your husband are attempting to stuff down angry feelings all the time, thinking that it is somehow sinful, you are headed down the wrong path. The Bible informs us that we will be angry, but commands that we should not sin. In other words, *fight right.* Stuffing anger is not a good way to handle the inevitability of relational discord. As a matter of fact, suppressed anger leads to increased levels of adrenaline and cortisol, which create undue stress on your body. Besides the fact that being angry makes you unhappy, all that irritation wreaks havoc on your body and your relationships.

Howard Markman, PhD, professor of psychology and head of the Center for Marital and Family Studies at the University of Denver, cites constructive arguing as the single biggest predictor of marital success over time.[1]

The reason anger is not a sin is because anger, at its root, is about being hurt. And getting your feelings hurt is not a sin. The truth is, if you are angry, you are wounded. Now you might be thinking, *No way! I get angry when my husband doesn't do the chores, but that doesn't mean I'm wounded. I'm just frustrated that he won't do them and has to be reminded to keep up with things.*

Well, let's dig deeper. Why do you think you feel frustrated? You desire help with certain chores, right? Having things done within a certain time frame is of value to you. So when he either refuses or forgets to do his chores, does the house get wounded? Does the house itself literally hurt because it is falling apart? Does the grass cry out when it sits un-mown? No—*you* are affected because you value the house being kept up and the lawn being mowed twice a month. Your husband's chipping in and doing his part helps *you*. And when he doesn't help, it hurts *you* because you are the one who cares about those things. By understanding that anger signals hurt, you can respond more logically in an argument and learn to fight right.

Examining Unexpressed Anger

Will and I had our share of these issues early in our marriage. We married when he was 23 and I was 21 (yes, we were babies—I shudder to imagine my 20-year-old getting married in a couple of years!). We were young and idealistic. We both had high standards for what we felt a "Christian marriage" should look like. As a matter of fact, Will came into marriage feeling as though we should never have conflict. On the other hand, I came in ready to throw it all out on the table every time there was a disagreement. The combination created a lot of communication difficulties. Because Will hated conflict, he ended up stuffing his feelings about many of the issues that made him hurt and angry. Now, it was great for me because I got to vent all I wanted, and he basically never said anything. And because he stuffed his feelings, I never even knew I was annoying and hurting him.

Anybody can become angry—that is easy, but to be angry
with the right person and to the right degree and at the right
time and for the right purpose, and in the right way—
that is not within everybody's power and is not easy.

—Aristotle

Maybe you're thinking that our situation wasn't so bad, but after a number of years Will just couldn't take all the stuff wadded up inside his soul. I will never forget going through marriage counseling and finding out Will had an abiding anger toward me. I was surprised—and devastated. Here I had been thinking all was well when, in reality, Will was growing more and more resentful because he was not expressing his real feelings—or his anger. It took some time for him to learn to express his anger, and it took even more time for me to learn to receive it, but learning to fight right was essential to strengthening our marriage.

So maybe you need to know: How do you fight right with your husband?

The One-Two Punch

The best Bible verses about fighting right are found in Ephesians 4:25-26: "Therefore each of you must put off falsehood and speak truthfully to his neighbor, for we are all members of one body. 'In your anger do not sin'" (*NIV*). These verses provide two key guidelines for fighting right. The first is to be honest and speak the truth. And the second is not to sin in anger. Both of these principles must be followed in order to fight right.

Marriage is meant to be the ultimate intimacy. It is about oneness. It is about loving unconditionally. The problem is that without authenticity, there is no intimacy. As a matter of fact, when I found out Will had been stuffing his feelings, I felt somewhat betrayed. While he felt he had been helping our marriage by not telling me he was angry, I felt as though he had been hiding his true self from me. Surprisingly, the very things he had kept to himself became some of the strongest cement for our marriage. When he shared the truth about how he felt about me as a wife and the issues he had with our marriage, we were brought closer together, rather than being driven apart.

Sound easy? Well, let me warn you that getting real doesn't mean life will be a cakewalk. Instead, expect to enter what we at our house fondly call "the tunnel of relational chaos." The tunnel of chaos is when one of you attempts to honestly report to the other the way you feel about the things that are happening in the marriage. In other words, you enter the tunnel when one of you decides to "speak truthfully and put off falsehood." Many times, this creates more fights—a real motivator, huh? So what to do with the fighting?

"Conflict," explains James Sniechowski, PhD, a couples counselor, "is generally understood to be either win or lose. And in that context, it's unattractive and dangerous. But conflict is in fact a signal from the relationship saying, 'Something has to change. Pay attention here.' And once you understand this, conflict can become the doorway to more intimacy in all areas: emotional, sexual, spiritual and intellectual."[2]

It's at this point that the second part of the Ephesians principle must be enacted. Verse 26 reads, "In your anger do not sin" (*NIV*). The *New Living Translation* says it this way: "Don't sin by letting anger gain control over you." The key is not allowing anger to have power over you, but instead choosing to manage how you handle the conflict. It's about learning to express your hurt or disappointment appropriately. It's about not stewing. It's about not screaming. It's about not demeaning. It's about all the things you already know to be true about how to treat people.

Really, you already know these things—but just imagine this: Let's say you arrange to meet with your minister to talk about a relationship problem in your life. And for you, it's a really big deal to make the appointment and ask for help. Now you're a little nervous, but when the day finally arrives, you're ready to tackle the issues. So you walk into his office for your meeting and after 15 minutes of waiting, you realize he is late. You are wondering what's going on but give him the benefit of the doubt—he's probably been detained by important business. When he finally arrives a few minutes later, you engage in a meaningful conversation in an attempt to get to the bottom of your problems. But as you converse with him, he says some things that hurt your feelings—he indicates that your problems stem from your attitudes. And although that might be the truth, it really wounds you and makes you mad.

Losing your temper causes a lot of trouble,
but staying calm settles arguments.
Proverbs 15:18, CEV

Now let me ask you a question: Would you even dare to let yourself scream at him? Would you ever in a million years call him an idiot? Would you storm out of his office, slamming the door as you go? I think not. Instead, I imagine you would use every reserve possible to keep a lid on your emotions. I think that no matter what he said, you would choose your words very carefully to avoid demeaning and humiliating him. The reason you would do that with your minister is because you know how to treat other people respectfully. You know how to feel angry and not sin. You know how to keep anger from controlling you. It's something you practice all the time with people you love a lot less than your husband. And it's something you must learn to practice with your husband if you want to enhance or even save your marriage.[3]

Recent studies reveal certain types of arguments between husbands and wives may actually weaken the immune system. But psychologist Janice Kiecolt-Glaser says, "We're not saying that people shouldn't disagree—it's the quality of the disagreement that seems to cause problems."[4]

Don't let the inevitable hurts and disappointments in life and marriage keep you from enjoying the sweet spots in your relationship. Instead, practice the fight-right principles in Ephesians and you both will win. You will have stuff to work through—just like any other married couple does—but you can do it with God's help. Start loving your man by becoming the best fighter of all, one who's honest and in control.

Loving Your Man

• List the top "hot topics" that create communication turmoil in your marriage.

• After listing the topics, identify the reasons why you feel they create arguments. For example, *Topic:* "Chores." *Reason:* "He never does them without my reminding him over and over. It's annoying and it makes me tired."

· Next, try to recognize the possible hurt you may be feeling as a result. For example, *I'm hurt because:* "I feel like he blows off my stuff. The house doesn't matter to him but it really matters to me. I don't feel like he cares about what I care about."

· List two ways to fight right in the above scenario, utilizing the Ephesians principles of truth and control.

· Think of a fight initiated by your husband in recent weeks. Can you identify his hurt in the situation? How can you use truth and control to fight right?

· Do you believe truth-telling might lead you into the tunnel of chaos? What would the payoff be?

· How could these godly guidelines change your marriage for the better?

e-Group

Up until a few months ago, Tuesday night was Fight Night at the Ehlers' house. Why Tuesday? Because Wednesday is trash day and taking out the trash is my husband, Blake's, job. Here's how it usually happened.

First, I announce cheerfully from the kitchen, "Trash day is tomorrow." Then I ask encouragingly a little while later, "Honey, would you please take the trash out tonight?" Later, although I can see the trash still sitting in the carport, I question, "Blake, did you take the trash out?" A few more minutes pass and I ask with a definite edge, "Have you taken out the trash, *yet?*" And then just before going to bed, I follow up with something like, "Why won't you just take out the trash?" and "You never help around the house—I have to do everything!" A gross exaggeration, but by this time I have worked myself into a huff and I go to bed upset, knowing that I'll be the one taking out the trash in the morning—again.

Today, I am a willing, uncomplaining trash taker-outer. Not because my husband is a slacker, and not because I suddenly like doing it, but because I have realized that the trash has never been about the trash—it's been about my wanting Blake to show his love by helping me with chores.

In the past, when he didn't do what I asked when I asked, I felt like he didn't appreciate me and my feelings got hurt. I am certain Blake had no idea that trash and love were connected that way. He just heard me asking him over and over again to take out the trash—and in an ever-increasing ugly tone of voice. So he responded in kind. No wonder he didn't drop everything and comply. Who would want to encourage my harpy-like behavior?

Reading this chapter has reminded me that getting angry is normal and that it's important to express anger. But I need to pick my battles. When the argument is worth it, I need to be honest and fair. When the issue is just not that important, I just need to let it go.

I still ask Blake to take out the trash sometimes (politely and only once), and he usually gets it out in a timely fashion. But if he forgets or just doesn't do it, I take the trash out. If we both forget, the trash sits in the storeroom until the next week—big deal. I'm not going to start another fight about the trash. Besides, I've found much more rewarding ways to encourage Blake's attention and appreciation on Tuesday evenings!

—Dee

Notes

1. Hara Estroff Marano, "The Reinvention of Marriage," *Psychology Today Magazine*, January/February 1992. http://www.psychologytoday.com/articles/index.php?term=pto-19920101-000032&page=3 (accessed April 2007).

2. "The Top 5 Things Couples Argue About," SixWise.com Newsletter, February 2006. http://www.sixwise.com/newsletters/06/02/22/the_top_5_things_couples_argue _about.htm (accessed April 2007).

3. If you are unable to control your anger when it comes to everyday issues, don't hesitate to see a counselor. Sometimes anger management issues are deep rooted and you may need a professional's help. There is no need to be embarrassed—just get some help so that you can start to enjoy a happier life and healthier relationships.

4. "From Bicker to Sicker," *Psychology Today Magazine*, January/February 1994. http:// www.psychologytoday.com/articles/pto-19940101-000003.html (accessed April 2007).

CHAPTER 3

Making Up with the Marlboro Man

Why Your Husband Really Is the Strong, Silent Type

Do you remember the Marlboro Man? He was the retro, hunky cowboy who wore a rugged red shirt, worked the range and rode his horse, all while a cigarette dangled from his mouth. Stoic yet rough and tumble, he was the image created for the Philip Morris Company in an effort to boost filtered cigarette sales back in the 1950s. The Marlboro Man and accompanying Marlboro Country are a part of one of the longest-running advertising campaigns of all time, securing a place in both American culture and commerce. This figure launched record sales for the company and had the staying power to instigate political action as recently as this year for promoting the successful sales of cigarettes. Jack Landry, the brand manager at Phillip Morris and creator of the Marlboro Man, explained why the image became a hugely successful commercial icon: "In a world that was becoming increasingly complex and frustrating for the ordinary man, the cowboy represented an antithesis—a man whose environment was simplistic and relatively pressure free. He was his own man in a world he owned."[1] What an interesting observation about men and society at large.

Now, I have a scenario for you to imagine. Let's say you and the Marlboro Man are married (possibly a stretch of the imagination), and then let's say he messes up (maybe he let's the cows eat all your purdy flowers), and the two of you have an argument. So your feelings are hurt, you're in need of an apology and he knows it. He's got his hat in his hands, he's taken out that dangling cigarette and he's just about to open his mouth to speak, more than ready to issue that much-needed apology.

But what does he say? Or rather, what do you expect him to say? If we're all being honest here, probably not much more than an uncomplicated, "I'm sorry, little darlin', about your purdy flowers." You wouldn't expect him to grovel or cry (never!) or make up some pretty poetry in order to fix the problem. You'd just accept his simple yet sincere apology and kiss his sweaty cheek, freeing him up to go catch those crazy cows on the range.

Why, you ask, do I put you through this fictitious silliness? Because, little darlin'—you *are* married to your very own Marlboro Man. Now wait, don't laugh! I mean it and here's why: The very thing Jack Landry said about men in the '50s is true of your man today. The world is truly "increasingly complex and frustrating for the ordinary man."

Seriously, let's take an honest look at the ongoing—and might I suggest *unrealistic*—expectations for men in our culture. On the one hand, we want them to be warriors in the workplace, able to rustle up a salary that would buy the whole open range. On the other hand, they should be sensitive, able to cuddle an infant and coo in appreciation of our amazing wifely abilities. And there is no greater madness than what is expected of men in marriage communication. While we desire manly decision-making and leadership in our spouse, we'd like a touchy-feely man when conflict comes along. It's a little crazy when you think about it.

A Marlboro Makeover

Just yesterday I was watching *Dr. Phil* while folding laundry. The episode was about a woman who was married to a self-professed male chauvinist pig (hereto after designated as Mr. SPMCP). This man was abrasive, cold and especially insensitive toward his wife. He enjoyed being the king of his castle and routinely bossed his poor wife around. He and his wife had submitted their marital issue to Dr. Phil, begging for his help to save their marriage. He agreed. That's how "The Divorce Experiment" episode came about: Dr. Phil had some "strong married women" move into the home with Mr. SPMCP to teach him a lesson by making him cook and clean and write sweet cards to his absent wife. (His real wife was shipped out to attend a women's empowerment event for a self-esteem boost.)

As I watched, I was stunned at the absolute rudeness of both the "strong married women" trying to reform Mr. SPMCP and Mr. SPMCP himself. And it made me think about the audacity of our society at large. Here it was, three o'clock in the afternoon, right about time for the kids to get home from school, and I turn on the TV to see this kind of weird junk. I continued watching (for research purposes only, of course) entranced, wondering what would eventually happen to Mr. SPMCP when Dr. Phil got a hold of him.

In just moments, Mr. SPMCP and his wife were reunited in front of the studio audience. Well, you can only imagine how the audience (99.98 percent of which was women) reacted when the man came out. They were ready to roast him. He walked on stage, saw his wife for the first time in weeks and gave her a long embrace. It kind of surprised me that while this guy had initially been intolerant of his wife and the strong women who were in his home, now that he was in front of his wife and Dr. Phil, he sounded genuinely humbled, ready to work on himself and the marriage. Numerous times, he asked for Dr. Phil's help to understand how and why he had acted the way he did toward his wife. It was truly astonishing to watch the helpless way he stuttered back and forth between his wife and Dr. Phil, carefully trying to answer questions, when all the while the audience was reacting in the background.

Here's the exchange between Dr. Phil and Mr. SPMCP as he reflected on his three days of suffering with the "strong married women" in charge of reforming him.

"Did you deserve it?" asked Dr. Phil.

"Absolutely," he responded, looking at his wife.

"Now what is your greatest fear at this point?" asked Dr. Phil.

"Losing my wife," he said, touching her arm.

I honestly thought that his wife, Dr. Phil and the audience would clap or cheer or something to encourage this man's heartfelt attempt to reconcile his nasty behavior. But surprisingly, Dr. Phil pressed on and on, asking more and more questions, until finally Mr. SPMCP blurted out, "You tell me. I don't know what I'm doing."[2]

When I heard that, I felt utter compassion. Not only because he had made an attempt to patch things up with his wife, but because Mr. SPMCP had also submitted himself to Dr. Phil and an audience of millions via television, all in an effort to set things right. It made me wonder why declaring his greatest fear—the fear of losing his wife—wasn't regarded as good enough. And then it made me wonder about the "complex and frustrating world for the ordinary man" so adeptly described by the Marlboro Man's creator.

The Magic Ingredient Every Man Needs

When I say that you are married to a Marlboro Man, I want you to understand that you're married to a *real man*. And real men are wired for and in need of deep, serious respect from their wives. Just like the original Marlboro Man, your man would love to have a "simplistic and relatively stress free environment," but he likely knows that marriage doesn't always add up to simple and stress free. He understands that there is always some turmoil and conflict in every relationship, but amidst the conflict, he still needs to be respected.

The problem is, however, that there is no greater capacity for disrespect in the relationship than during conflict between a husband and wife (just watch *Dr. Phil!*). When you launch into in an argument, there is a fine line between "telling the truth in love" and an all-out attack on your spouse's tender spot. For men, that tender spot of vulnerability is respect. During conflict it's important that truth-telling doesn't lessen your respect for him—doesn't negatively affect how he is viewed in your eyes—which I know can be difficult, especially if you feel angry.

Dr. Eggerich, the founder of Love and Respect Ministries, contends that marital conflict makes most men feel disrespected because it is not often handled in a respectful fashion. He says, "Men need to feel respected during conflict more than they need to feel loved. This does not mean men do not need love . . . men know deep down that their wives love them, but they are not at all that sure that their wives respect them."[3] So why in the world are men so "respect-sensitive"? Dr. Eggerich describes it here:

> I believe that men hold respect and honor as almost equal values. My experience as a man, with other men, tells me that in our arena we have an honor code and if we don't live by that code, we're in for big trouble. We have learned from boyhood that there are certain things you just don't do, certain things you just don't say. A woman will talk to a husband in the home in the way that a man would never talk to him. He can't believe she can be so belligerent, so disrespectful.[4]

Aside from your husband's desire for respect, the appeal for respect in the marriage relationship is biblical. Ephesians 5:33

says, "So again I say, each man must love his wife as he loves himself, and the wife must respect her husband." Now maybe you're feeling a little defensive now, because I seem to be insinuating that there's disrespect involved when you and your husband fight. While it might seem unfair of me to assume that, in my experience (and the experience among many of my married friends), I know it happens all too often. Sometimes in my attempt to "work things out" and "get to the bottom of the problem," I unintentionally dishonor Will by failing to remember that my idea of respectful is not often the same as Will's idea. Here's what I mean.

Recently, Will and I had an argument because he had been out late a lot due to church meetings. His time away at night had negatively impacted both our family time and our communication. While Will is usually extremely sensitive about our family time in the evening, over the course of several weeks he had been gone several nights in a row. Not only did this make him tired, but it also made us cranky with each other.

During this time, a hot topic came up that needed resolution, and I launched into the discussion, desiring to resolve the conflict. Will stood at the door to our bedroom listening quietly. Just when I was about to hit on what I felt was the key issue, he shook his head suddenly and said tensely, "I can't talk to you like this." And then he walked out. Typically I would have followed him into the next room with a "Hey, wait a minute!" and continued the discussion, but honestly, I just felt too tired to mess with it. Instead, I put on my tennis shoes and went for a walk at dusk. I walked up and down the streets in our neighborhood, crying and feeling very sorry for myself thinking, *Will won't talk to me.*

When I got back, I settled in on the curb, hugging my knees, letting the night envelop my sadness. Within minutes, Will walked up behind me, apologized and asked if I wanted to talk. We sat on the curb together and rationally discussed the problem and his schedule. I also shared with him how it really bothered me that he had walked out during the conflict. And he in turn told me that he had felt really irritated by my accusatory tone. He told me he had walked out because he didn't want to add another problem to the pile. And so my "pity party" walk had provided two things: time and space for both of us to get a little saner about the situation.

Where Have All the Cowboys Gone?

What I didn't understand for nearly 20 years of marriage but am becoming increasingly aware of is this: Men often withdraw in marital conflict because it is overwhelming to them. Some days, your man might come home from his "complex world" only to find conflict at home. If a wife is attacking her husband with a barrage of words, he is likely to feel as though his wife doesn't think too much about his ability to be a respectable man. And though he wouldn't likely say so in words, this is painful for him. Literally. It has actually been documented that men have a physiological response that is much different from that of women when it comes to communication conflict in marriage. A man's heart races and his blood pressure spikes substantially more than a woman's during an argument, which results in an increase in his antagonistic feelings. When a man experiences his wife's launching into a conflict full speed ahead, he often flees emotionally (shuts down or stonewalls or walks out) instead of fights, because he is attempting to handle his feelings and maintain the "code of honor."

When I realized that some of Will's reactions were part of his attempt to handle the escalating conflict and manage his emotions, I came to understand, once again, that I don't always get everything that is going on in his head. In the past, I routinely interpreted his walking out as not being willing to resolve an issue, or as attempting to end a conversation. Now I have come to realize with all clarity that I can't understand everything Will is thinking, and so I cautiously guard against thinking I know it all where he is concerned. Instead, I seek to understand his behavior and motives by discussing them with him. It's a dedicated move on my part to be a lifelong learner where my husband is concerned—and to always give him the benefit of the doubt, which he most certainly deserves from me, of all people.

Someone's thoughts may be as deep as the ocean,
but if you are clever, you will discover them.
Proverbs 20:5, *CEV*

Last week reminded me of how often we lose sight of the Marlboro Man we married. I picked up the phone to hear a friend of mine crying uncontrollably. She and her husband had just had a horrible fight, complete with excessive yelling and name-calling. She told me through her tears that just as her husband had attempted to storm out the door, she stopped him by vigorously grabbing his arm. When he went to pull his arm from her, she lost her footing and landed on the ground. She was completely devastated because he had angrily left the house without checking on her well-being or resolving the conflict.

When I talked her through the situation (and recommended marriage counseling), I advised her that in the future she should probably let her husband walk out the door instead of physically trying to stop him. Why? Because he had likely been doing all he could in the situation. I know that her husband is a good man and he really loves his wife. But I also know that he is a *man* and that he probably regarded his leaving as a last resort at the time—he knew he needed to get out of the situation as quickly as possible without letting his emotions rage up inside. It was probably the best option for him at that moment because the "code of honor" had been violated. Here was a conflict in which his wife had demeaned him. (Remember the name-calling?) He had likely wanted to defend himself because he'd been loudly disrespected (she admits to this) and deeply wounded. And while I am not advocating that walking away from conflict is always the best option, in some situations allowing a man a little space to resolve emotional conflict is a good idea.

As women, we often feel the need to press through the difficulties verbally and get back to that "mushy-gooshy" feeling that makes us feel loved and connected. For us, more words equal more resolution and ultimately more love. But for a man, the process of resolving a conflict and making up is not always the same. Making up for a man might mean fixing things up with as little disrespect and dirty-laundry airing as possible. For a man, the harder a woman digs into the problem (especially when it comes to something she feels her husband has done wrong), the more insecure he feels. And the crazy thing is that the more insecure he feels, the more distance he will put between himself and his wife—not at all what a woman is shooting for here.

Making Up with Him in Mind

We need to revisit the hunky cowboy you married. You know—the strong, *silent* type. While you will have communication conflict in marriage, it doesn't have to be a negative thing. If you can show some respect during the conflict, I would bet you'd get far more than you ever bargained for when it comes to positive results and more of that lovey-dovey feeling. Since the ultimate goal of resolving a conflict and making up is about mending hurt and disagreement, you have the power to minimize the hurt by acting and reacting in ways that honor your husband and God. Respectfully. You have the power to shorten the conflict and help your husband feel honored in the process. Your part is thinking through your tone, your nonverbal cues, your word choices and your timing. All those things matter.

What's the bottom line here? Understanding a man's deep need for respect is a huge step in the right direction to equip yourself as you deal with the inevitable issues of conflict—and seek to make up with your real man.

Loving Your Man

- Why is respecting your husband during conflict one of the most essential ingredients in making up?

- If your husband typically stonewalls, shuts down or walks out during your arguments, can you identify areas of disrespect on your part? How might changing your way of handling conflict affect his communication with you?

- Is there a difference between stonewalling, shutting down or walking out—and a complete lack of emotional authenticity? How can you tell the difference? (Chapter 2 identifies stuffing feelings or the inability to be authentic during conflict.)

- During conflict, we all desire to have the last word. How does that mindset hinder your ability to mend the relationship? What's behind the need to have the final word?

- Actor Michael J. Fox said of his relationship with his wife, Tracy, "What it really comes down to for us is cutting each other some slack—this is the one person who's going to give you a break. Maybe point out that you screwed up, but ultimately give you a pass."[5] How hard is it to give your husband "a pass"? How does Michael's perspective give you an inside look at the way men view making up?

• Is there an expectation among women for a man to respond like a woman when it comes to handling conflict and making up? Is that a reasonable expectation?

• How is your accepting a simple "I'm sorry" at face value of great importance to your husband?

• There might be times you unintentionally dishonor your husband. How does the Bible teach us to handle the problem of unintentional sin?

e-Group

I *hated* this chapter. I hated this chapter because I loathed what I saw in me after I read it. It was as if Susie had been lurking around our house during arguments, taking notes. When I argue with my husband, I want to talk—get it all out in the open and do it *now*! I feel like my husband should stop, listen to me, ignore all the barbs I have thrown his way and completely see my point of view.

After reading the chapter, I finally understand why he leaves the room when we argue. And why he grows quiet—actually, he grows quieter and quieter as I grow louder and louder. It now makes sense why he pulls away when I hold on to his arm in an argument. I never understood why he couldn't "shake it off" after our disagreements, but now I know that I wounded him where it matters most. Without realizing it, I was showing him utter contempt and disrespect. It was never my intention to treat him this way, to scar him this way. Understanding this chapter made me reevaluate how I fight with Steve. It made me realize he has Marlboro Man tendencies—and it created a desire on my part to honor him more. Susie's insights made me feel instantly tender toward my husband.

—Liz

Notes

1. Kathleen Schalch, "Present at the Creation: The Marlboro Man," *Morning Edition*, National Public Radio, October 21, 2002. http://www.npr.org/programs/morning/features/patc/marlboroman/ (accessed April 2007).
2. "The Divorce Experiment," *The Dr. Phil Show*, episode 731. http://drphil.com/shows/show/731/ (accessed April 2007).
3. Dr. Eggerich, *Love and Respect* (Nashville, TN: Thomas Nelson Publishers, 2004), p. 56.
4. Ibid., p. 57.
5. Roberta Caploe, "The Ties That Bind: An Interview with Michael J. Fox," *Ladies Home Journal*, September 2006. http://www.lhj.com/lhj/story.jhtml?storyid=/templatedata/lhj/story/data/1157487991679.xml (accessed April 2007).

CHAPTER 4

Vive la Différence!

How to Appreciate That Your Husband Responds Like a Man

For a writer, waiting to land a publisher is an awful lot like a woman desperately wanting to get pregnant. In the writer's case, you do everything you know to do in an attempt to conceptualize your brilliant idea. First, you craft perfect sample chapters, then painstakingly fulfill the obligatory proposal and finally prayerfully submit the manuscript in its entirety to your agent, who in turn sends out a mass email to multiple publishing houses. Then you wait and wait.

It is an achingly long process, filled with alternating feelings of naïve hope and crushing despair. With every tidbit of interest from a publisher comes the test, most often resulting in a false positive and more waiting. Excruciating waiting. And wondering, *Did my idea make any creative connection at all? Will any publisher help birth this oh-so-important manuscript? Will the world ever hear this important message? Won't someone give life to this literary baby?* Let a couple of months like that roll by for an aspiring author and the wait will just about kill any confidence she has in her abilities.

This was exactly where I was when I approached my husband for some spiritual and emotional support: I had two "babies" floating around in various stages of pre-publication, neither of which had yet landed a contract. On the brink of mental and artistic annihilation, I needed some understanding and encouragement. My sense of dejection led me straight to my husband, who is both a pastor and an author. Just months before he had *finally* landed a book contract, Will had ridden the mad roller-coaster ride of rejection and dejection—until finally a publisher had decided to champion his book, *Pray Big*. So of all the people I knew, he could feel my pain.

Seeking sympathy, I walked into the study, leaned carelessly against the wall and heaved a sigh. My glumness filled the room. He looked up and quietly waited until I had completed my litany of disappointments concerning my writing, my ministry and my life as I knew it. He listened with particular care and thoughtfulness. Looking at him and thinking of the months past when he had suffered through his waiting, I just knew that something tender and hopeful would flow from his lips to light my way through the darkness. And then I heard, "Hey, why don't you go to the grocery store and buy some bread?"

I furrowed my brow and leaned forward, confused. "What?"

"Yeah, it might make you feel better to go and spend some money . . ." his voice trailed off as he noticed my reaction.

"*Are you suggesting that I go to the store and buy some bread?*" I was shocked and surprised, caught off guard by this idea.

"Well, I was just thinking . . ." ever so slowly he was awakening to the effect of his words, "that spending money might make you feel better."

"I cannot believe that you are telling me *you think buying bread is retail therapy*. You are asking me to make a grocery store run when I am in the middle of a life and literary breakdown!"

Fortunately for him, his comments on my situation made me laugh. But after I caught my breath, I confronted his monstrous lack of tact. His complete lack of understanding. His unpleasant suggestion that errand-running would help my mood. He was extraordinarily lucky that it was a stable time of the month for me.

What He Thinks and How You Feel

When situations like this arise, there are two important truths I must remember so that I don't become a hysterical ninny, tears and all. The first: *My husband is a man; therefore, he thinks and talks like a man.* And the second: *I am not a man; therefore, I don't think and talk like a man.*

Sometimes I wonder if men and women really suit each other. Perhaps they should live next door and just visit now and then.

—Katherine Hepburn

Let's face it, men and women are created differently. If I had talked with a girlfriend that day when I was experiencing ministry blues, she likely would have listened intently and tried to empathize with what I was feeling. We would have been chatting it up, sharing feelings in common. Why? Because women largely operate with "feel first" language skills. We are wonderfully intuitive about the feelings of others when communicating. Women tend to sympathize and empathize easily, and even when we don't, we know enough about interpersonal relationships to *act* like it.

Men, on the other hand, largely operate using "think first" language skills. They are more likely to manage communication mentally rather than emotionally. They gloss over the verbal details and analyze the content of a conversation in light of problem solving.

Of course, there are exceptions to these generalizations, but they don't change the fact that men and women have vastly different communication techniques that seem to be innate. And although it's not completely unheard of for a man to react as a "feel first" communicator, you're setting yourself up for heartache if you expect this reaction all the time. The truth is, while men are able to navigate "feel first," their instinctive response will most often be "think first."

The average woman uses 7,000 words a day and five tones of speech. The average man uses 2,000 words and three tones.[1]

Remembering the "think first" response of men is important because it impacts how they relate. For example, men don't typically chit-chat on the phone for hours, they don't analyze a coworker's conversation to pieces, and they don't delve deep into the way they *feel.* Of course, we know this to be true of men—experience and common sense have taught us that this is exactly how men communicate. And yet, if you're like me, you struggle to implement this knowledge in your marriage. Why? *Because our desire to be understood is often greater than our desire to understand.*

If you are only looking at marriage communication as a way to feel understood, you miss the opportunity to enhance the relationship by understanding. For example, if I had solely focused on Will's advice to run to the grocery store when I was having my little breakdown, I would have been very angry with him. But because it was a good day at the Davises and I could laugh at what Will suggested, I was able to look beyond my self-centered focus and hear what my "think first" husband had to say. His comments were motivated by a desire to distract me from my melancholy musing. He heard the rumblings, knowing that I often focus too much on the "whys" of life, and in typical male form, he was moving to the solution side of the equation. In the situation, even though my "feel first" skill set was prompting me to react defensively and angrily, I paused long enough to remember Will was just responding like a man.

Dr. Laura Schlessinger gets it right when she describes how women so often forget that the men in their lives communicate, well, like men.

> The first thing I usually remind women who call complaining about the communication problems with their husbands is that the callers are probably not even communicating but using their husbands as girlfriends or shrinks; the husbands are supposed to show interest, agree, and remain uncritical and unchallenging. Husbands imagine (so foolishly) that their wives are telling them something they actually need to know because they're supposed to do something about it. Otherwise, the men can't imagine why the "communication" is happening at all.[2]

Author and psychologist John Gray, of *Men Are from Mars, Women Are from Venus* fame, explains the communication discrepancy using the "alien theory" of relationships:

> There's a fun way to look at our relationships. During those moments when you want to pull your hair out, when you wonder what's going wrong, why this isn't working out, and you think maybe we're not right for each other, maybe we're just too different, that's the time to remember that maybe your partner is from another planet. Men are from Mars and women are from Venus and on these planets we have different customs. If you learn to honor and respect the customs of the different planets, then things go smoothly, but if you don't honor and respect the customs, you step on each other's toes.[3]

Those "customs" he talks about don't require a degree in human psychology to understand. It's nothing more than basic biology—or *boy*ology, as I like to call it—and the main premise is: Men and women are created in uniquely different ways.

What's my point here? If you want to revolutionize your marriage, start expecting your husband to act, think and speak like a man—not a woman.

Accepting the Differences

When I think about the fact that I have been married to Will for over 20 years and yet I am still taken aback by his male responses, it amazes me. In truth, I wonder if I will ever understand men in general and my man in particular. It truly is remarkable how they think and operate just because of their maleness.

Women have a greater facility for language than men do and when women are under stress or in difficulty, their brains secrete much higher levels of a chemical called oxycontin than men's brains do. Its effect is to drive women to the company of other people for intense discussion.[4]

I truly want to understand Will, with God's help, because that is when I will really begin to delight in my marriage—and in return be a delight to Will. Here is the bottom line (and this isn't rocket science): I must accept Will as a wonderfully designed *human* who is wholly different from me and appreciate him as he is—created by God. And if I want to *truly* delight in my marriage, I must acknowledge the way he complements me in my weakness . . . because who else would have the guts to suggest that I run errands in the middle of a moody breakdown?

Marriage, at its heart, is a breathtaking way to understand the big "God picture" in life. God completely accepts me because of Jesus Christ. He's not waiting on me to get my act together. He's not waiting for me to become more God-like before He'll listen to me. Instead, He sees me and embraces me right where I am. My whole relationship with God is based on God's looking at me, realizing my need and launching into action. God sent the ultimate communicator, Jesus Christ, to concretely show His unconditional acceptance and love for me.

And Jesus models in my life what I am expected to do for others—and especially for Will. I should love and accept my husband as God loves and accepts me: *unconditionally*. While we could get all riled up and discuss gender differences for hours, that really isn't the point. Although it is wise to work at understanding your spouse and all his masculine tendencies, at the end of the day you just need to accept him—like God has accepted you. Our ability to lovingly accept each other in marriage is part of God's desire and plan for us. Romans 15:7 says it this way: "So accept each other just as Christ has accepted you; then God will be glorified."

Self-Improvement at the Other's Expense

See, the thing is, we need other people. But of course, the problem with needing other people is that they can be so very annoying. Really, think about it. Just about the time you start feeling like you've got it together spiritually, say right after you've read your Bible first thing in the morning, someone in your house (okay, we're talking about your husband) goes and wakes up and does something that bothers you. And then after he bothers you, you end up lashing out and saying or doing something rude. Then you feel bad, thinking that if he weren't around, perhaps you would find it easier to be the awesome spiritual person you and God hope you'll be.

*Getting along with men isn't what's truly important. The vital
knowledge is how to get along with a man, one man.*
—Phyllis McGinley

The real problem with this is that God isn't "into" that
kind of spiritual plan. The fact that you *feel* spiritual because
you read the Bible doesn't have anything to do with whether
you're really *being* spiritual. Being spiritual is about living life
in the real world—with all those people wrecking your awesome picture of yourself. It's about living among those people, loving and accepting them, and thereby glorifying God in
your life.

Those "annoying people" in my life can act as refining agents
if I allow them. When I think I am kind but I don't have patience
with my husband, am I kind? When I think I am wise, but I don't
think before I speak, am I wise? It's tricky, isn't it? If I'm alone, I
don't have to worry myself with any such thing as sanctification
("sanctification" is just a big, scary, religious-sounding word that
means to be made more like Jesus). But it is what marriage does
to you, should you be willing to let it. Marriage pulls you out of
yourself, possibly kicking and screaming, so that your heart is
enlarged to love.

When you are at the edge with your husband, believing that he
just doesn't get it, pray and ask for God's help to love him, admit-
ting that your thinking is part of the problem. When you feel alone
and your husband won't listen, pray and ask for God's help to love
him, knowing that God is there to listen even when your husband isn't. When you want to end it all, believing that your
husband isn't worth all the energy or the time, pray and ask for
God's help to love him, accepting that you aren't always especially worthy either. You solve the need by *loving* instead of

seeking love—and that's very Jesus-like. You solve the need by *understanding* instead of *seeking to be understood*—again, very Jesus-like. What God did for each of us is what we must strive to do for our husbands.

If God uses my sweet man to open my eyes to more of who He is and how He loves me, I am humbled. If God uses my marriage to make me more like Him, I will be grateful. And if I can become more loving and accepting of the people in my life by accepting God's design to sanctify me through marriage, so be it.

Who but God could have thought up a more beautiful way to bless us than in letting us learn to love one another? By learning to understand instead of being understood? And so, in all earnestness, I say, "*Vive la différence!*"

Loving Your Man

- Does your husband exhibit different communication styles from your own? Is he is a "think first" or "feel first" communicator? What about you?

- How do your differing communication styles create conflict in your marriage?

- What are the benefits of having someone in your life who doesn't always think and talk just like you?

- How is God's original plan for marriage a part of His "big picture" plan for your life and the life of your spouse? Why do you think God set it up that way?

- Think of three instances in which God used your marriage to sanctify you as an individual. What are the three things God has taught you about you, your husband and Himself?

e-Group

I laughed out loud when I read the story about the bread. What a man thing to say!

The "think first" concept was very hard for me to accept at first. I lived on my own for so long that I was used to solving my own problems. And I have to admit, the need that my husband, David, has to "fix" my problems does, at times, drive me absolutely crazy. In fact, I used to turn away or ignore him whenever he tried to suggest a solution. I mean, honestly, did he think I hadn't thought of that? (I hadn't.)

However, recently I made a discovery: Sometimes my husband sees things from a whole different perspective—one that I might never have pursued. Sometimes, if I'll take a moment and actually listen to him, I'll find that his words hold great wisdom.

And I couldn't agree more with Susie when she says that God uses the people in her life to refine her. I see every day that God is using David to refine me and make me more like Jesus. He's used him to help me learn to hold my tongue. He's used him to teach me to pray first and act second. I've discovered that this whole "feel first" mindset that we women embrace can often get us into a lot of trouble. Not that I don't often still feel first and think later—it's just that now I'm more aware of how my "feeling first" often affects and even hurts the people around me.

Of course, some days I still wish my husband would get mad with me over an injustice or wallow with me over some heartbreak. But most of the time, I am glad for my man's "think first" heart, because it is teaching me to see my world through a whole new set of eyes.

—Julie

Notes
1. Hara Estroff Marano, "Secrets of Married Men," *Psyched for Success*, July 26, 2004. http://www.psychologytoday.com/articles/pto-20040726-000013.html (accessed April 2007).
2. Laura Schlessinger, *The Proper Care and Feeding of Husbands* (New York: HarperCollins Publishers Inc., 2004), p. 94.
3. John Gray, *Men, Women, and Relationships: Making Peace with the Opposite Sex* (Hillsboro, OR: Beyond Words Publishing, 1993), p. x.
4. Marianne J. Legato and Laura Tucker, *Why Men Never Remember and Women Never Forget* (New York: Rodale Books, 2005), p. 105.

The Garden of Disenchantment

Did you hear? Supermodel Kate Moss has created a surefire way to stay out of the marital Garden of Disenhantment even *before* she ties the knot with her fiancé rocker Pete Doherty. Apparently, she has made a list of six rules that he must obey or she will call off their wedding. She insists he must stop flirting with groupies and using drugs, end contact with his "loser" friends, start eating properly, begin writing poetry daily and call her at least three times a day. She is calling the new rules "Kate's Commandments" and instituting them because, as one source said, "Pete is prone to going AWOL."[1]

While Kate's rules seem a bit absurd (I'm thinking she should aim higher), most women are constantly tempted to try molding their man's behavior. And though you might not worry about your husband going AWOL or concern yourself with his lack of poetry writing, having your very own set of "commandments" might sound appealing. I mean, wouldn't it be great to create your own guidelines for marriage? You know, a list of things your husband should and shouldn't do in order to chase away the irritations that gnaw away at your relationship. How about these for starters?

- Thou shalt not leave your dirty clothes lying on the floor.
- Thou shalt not get angry about how much money I spend at the mall.

· Thou shalt not hunt, golf or waterski every weekend.

· Thou shalt listen with interest whenever I feel like talking.

· Thou shalt cheerfully participate in all household chores.

· Thou shalt romance with no sexual intent.

Things would be much easier if he would comply! Then the marriage would be lovely and dreamy and honeymoony again—or would it? In this section, we'll take an honest look at some of the topics that seem to have the greatest capacity for irritation in relationships, and then hear what God has to say about that man you married.

Note

1. "Kate Moss' marriage rules for Doherty" *Life Style Extra*: Showbiz News for October 16, 2006. http://www.lse.co.uk/ShowbizNews.asp?Code=RL165034E&headline=kate_moss_marriage_rules_for_doherty (accessed May 2007).

Chapter 5

Missing Prince Charming?

Why Disillusionment in Marriage Doesn't Mean You Married a Toad

Post-wedding blues. A growing number of brides are suffering from them, according to TheNest.com. Apparently, brides everywhere are getting a real thrill out of all the prep and planning involved in throwing a party for the big day and then waking with the blues after all is said and done. Lee Madden, a psychologist, sums up the problem: "Getting married is a party. Being married isn't as glamorous. You don't get to be a star all the time."[1]

Isn't that the truth? You certainly realize you aren't a star when you wake up to find you are married to a regular guy who forgets to throw his dirty socks in the hamper and you're in charge of cleaning them. It's a common occurrence. As a matter of fact, the post-wedding blues are really just a sign that the honeymoon is over. And it's something married people have been waking up to for generations.

If you had any expectations regarding marriage at all and are still married, then it's likely you have come to accept some disillusionment as part of the package. If you haven't felt the sting of dashed expectations, then it is likely that you are reading this book on the white sandy beaches of Hawaii with your newlywed husband at your side. (Just put the book down and go frolic in the surf—there will be plenty of time for this chapter later.)

Now honestly, the only other option that might have kept you from the occasional feeling of disillusionment in marriage is the possibility that you set the bar for your marriage very low. Perhaps you never hoped your husband would make you happy. You never dreamed of marital bliss as a little girl. You never crossed your fingers and wished to marry Prince Charming, while tenderly tearing petals off a daisy, "He loves me . . . he loves me not." And yet setting the bar low, while it might spare you disappointment, is not an especially attractive philosophy of marriage in my mind—though apparently it's the world's best hope. In an article in *Psychology Today*, Aviva Patz reports findings from Ted Huston, PhD, a professor of human ecology and psychology at the University of Texas at Austin. Dr. Huston conducted a long-term study of married couples in a quest to understand marital happiness and long-term viability. The results were a little startling and disheartening for those of us who dream of living "till death do us part" with our Prince Charming. Patz reports:

> First, contrary to popular belief, Huston found that many newlyweds are far from blissfully in love. Second, couples whose marriages begin in romantic bliss are particularly divorce-prone because such intensity is too hard to maintain. Believe it or not, marriages that start out with less "Hollywood romance" usually have more promising futures. Accordingly, and this is the third major finding, spouses in lasting but lackluster marriages are not prone to divorce, as one might suspect; their marriages are less fulfilling to begin with, so there is no erosion of a Western-style romantic ideal.[2]

Wow! There's so much sunshine there I barely know where to start!

First, the findings report that romantic bliss creates unbearable intensity. Okay, knock out romantic bliss. Second, the study suggests that a lackluster marriage will act as a deterrent for divorce. You hear that, girls? Just keep those standards low. Don't hope for much. And if you dare to feel a little inspired in your marriage—just pop that balloon of motivation, thereby deflating all momentum, or else you're headed for divorce. Whatever you do, make sure and keep that love lackluster. Whew.

The Problem with a Perfect Prince Charming

The world's best findings are no match for what God intends in marriage. Could I venture to suggest that God intends for us to enjoy both a realistic Prince Charming and a long-lasting union? He does—and such a reality can happen in your life. But only with God's help. To get to the place of living with your real-life Prince Charming, you have to accept some help from God's Word in order to gain the proper perspective, because every Prince Charming is just a man, from head to toe, and every marriage is full of imperfections, start to finish.

When God created marriage, He did so for companionship and completeness. God made Eve for Adam so that he wouldn't be alone and so that he would have help in life. Genesis 2:18 says, "And the LORD God said, 'It is not good for the man to be alone. I will make a companion who will help him.'" From God's point of view, marriage is about companionship and working together. It is not necessarily all about getting your needs met. (But . . .) It is not necessarily all about how you feel. (Hey now!) And marriage is certainly not all about being the center of attention. (Rats!) I love how the psychologist carefully phrased it: "You don't get to be a star all the time." This is psychobabble for, "You gotta get over yourself."

See, stardom is all about *me, me, me,* while marriage is all about *we, we, we.* The very basis of the relationship is the focus on togetherness over and above the focus on self. Now, to the extent that your Prince Charming is enhancing the *we* part of your marriage, celebrate. To the extent that your Prince Charming *isn't* enhancing the *me* part of your marriage—well, you gotta get over yourself because that's where disillusionment about marriage sets in.

Let me illustrate: Will and I had been married about 10 years when I finally realized he wasn't perfect (I know, I know—we had a *really* long honeymoon period). It was a time in my life when I awakened to his imperfections and found he wasn't making me "happy." I spent several months moping in the garden of disenchantment and then realized I had two choices: Either I could become "unhappy" in my marriage, or I could change my idea of what my Prince Charming was there for in the first place.

As I prayed through the problem with God, I came to understand one of the main issues: I had been expecting something from marriage that God had never promised. God didn't promise Will would be there to make me happy. Will wasn't there to be a fictionalized Prince Charming, able to fix all of my needs and fulfill the deep desires of my heart. Instead, he was there to be a companion in this life we created together, children and all. See, the problem with expecting our Prince Charming to rescue us on the white horse is . . . it's not his job. It's God's job. And when I figured that out, it changed my attitude toward Will and our marriage.

The Princess and the Problem

In the first decade of our marriage, Will pretty much fit the Prince Charming image. He came into our marriage with a "will work for love" mentality that fit in quite well with the rescuing-hero persona. And I, as a young wife, had a fair amount of "princess" baggage and was quite willing to let him labor for my favor. While Will managed to work hard at keeping up his princely image, scoring points by serving me, I enjoyed basking in the *me, me, me* mentality.

We all suffer from the preoccupation that there exists . . .
in the loved one, perfection.
—Sidney Poitier

But since he was a human prince and not a fictionalized storybook prince, Will finally got tired. And when he did, he couldn't get on that white horse to rescue me from my disillusionment. As a result, I fell into a pit of despair. I wandered in gloomy desolation over my romantic notions, my life and marriage in general. Where was my Prince Charming—had he turned into a toad? As time went on and Will still did not rescue me from my gloom and doom, I skidded into ambivalence. My thoughts about our marriage were depressing: *Would I forever be relegated to lowering my standards, settling for what I felt was a lackluster marriage? Would Will ever get back on the horse and come to my aid? What was I to do with the forlorn feelings swarming our relationship?*

In the chamber tower of my heart, I found an answer to my question. Early one morning, I discovered these words in my Bible:

> For your Creator will be your husband. The LORD Almighty is his name! He is your Redeemer, the Holy One of Israel, the God of all the earth. For the Lord has called you back from your grief—as though you were a young wife abandoned by her husband (Isa. 54:5-6).

When I read the verse, I wept—I realized I had completely missed God's rightful place in my life. As I cried out to God, I began to see that only He could rescue me from my disillusionment

and only He could make my marriage what it needed to be. For
all the years I'd been expecting Will to be my Prince Charming,
I had denied God the opportunity to be my first husband—and
my first love.

What I began to realize was that my love for Will slowly
had displaced my love for God. My hope in Will exceeded my
hope in God. I wanted Will to fulfill my needs in a way that
only God could, and as long as I counted on Will for my happiness and fulfillment, God was relegated to being an extra
in the story of my love life. I had counted on Will for my happiness, my strength, my security. And in the process of making Will into a fictionalized hero-husband, I had squeezed
God out of His rightful role in our marriage. And the truth
is, when God is squeezed out of marriage, marriage doesn't
work well.

To Complete or Compete?

See, God did not make Eve to *compete* for a place in Adam's
heart; He made Eve to *complete* a place in his heart. And the
same went with Adam for Eve. The principle has extreme appli-
cation where marriage is concerned, because to the extent
that your love for and dependence on your husband compete
with your love for and dependence on God, *your husband is an
idol in your life*. God doesn't do well with idols in our lives. He
gets pretty offended when we let even the good things and
people in our lives compete for His attention. Exodus 20:5
tells us how strongly God feels about misplaced devotion: "I,
the Lord your God, am a jealous God who will not share your
affection with any other god!" And the problem with idolatry
is that the natural consequence for placing love and devotion
in the wrong person or thing creates unbearable heartache
and trauma.

Yet I hold this against you: You have forsaken your first love.
Revelation 2:4, *NIV*

Now maybe you're thinking you have not made your husband into a "god." But consider this question: Do you expect him to provide for you in the ways that only God can? Have you unintentionally placed your husband, instead of God, on the throne of your heart? Are you counting on your husband to fix your unhappiness? Your insecurities? Do you depend on him for your "daily bread"? Those are all things only God can provide. While He can give you those things *through* your husband, He certainly must get the credit for it. Your marriage is a generous gift from God, meant to complete you but not to compete with the Giver.

If you have set up your husband as an unreal, fictionalized Prince Charming, you will be disappointed and "unhappy" in your marriage. No one besides God can truly meet your needs. If you give away your greatest love and devotion to anyone other than God, all others will suffer—including your sweet Prince Charming.

Invite your husband off the high horse of your greatest expectations and settle into living shoulder to shoulder with the man God gave you in marriage. If you want a real-life Prince Charming, then willingly relinquish your desire for him to be anything other than what God intended him to be: a man who completes and helps you in life. In the process of letting your earthly husband be a real guy, warts and all, your marriage will bloom into the kind of relationship it was intended to be—one that is romantic, exhilarating and ready to realize some God-sized potential.

Loving Your Man

- In what ways do you lean into your husband, expecting him to make you happy?

- What are the areas of life that most often make you unhappy where your husband is concerned? How are the areas that bother you God's responsibility rather than your husband's?

- Is there a chance that your expectations for your husband really are a symptom of idolatry in your life? Is there a chance the natural repercussions of idolatry are creating havoc in your marriage? How?

- What are the blessings of having companionship in marriage? Is there a balance between completeness in your marriage and dependence on God?

- Does your husband ever look like the toad rather than the prince? Can you give reasons why you sometimes see him like that?

- Honestly, do you have more of a *me*-centered outlook or a *we*-centered outlook in your marriage? What are three things you can begin to do to get a *we*-centered mindset in your marriage?

e-Group

As a new bride, this chapter seemed to be written for me, a warning of sorts. You see, I was one of those girls who grew up thinking that my future husband would ultimately make me happy. And so when I found myself at the age of 25, with *all* of my friends married and seemingly happy, I faced the realization that maybe I wouldn't be getting married right away (or at all). *How could I possibly be happy on my own?* I wondered. Yet I didn't want to spend my life in misery.

I made a decision. I decided to put my life in the hands of the One who I knew already loved me completely—Jesus Christ. I set about figuring out how to let God be my joy, my happiness, my strength. It was because of that decision, when I married at the age of 28, that I had no delusions about a Prince Charming coming to save me. Now though, as I bask in my own honeymoon period with a man I love deeply and who *does* at times look and feel a little like Prince Charming, this chapter warns me of how easy it is to put my hope in my husband instead of in my God. I find myself tempted every day to put my hope in the man who sometimes makes me breakfast and often whispers sweet things in my ear. My husband is tangible. I can feel him, see him and hear him. It's easy to put my hope in him.

This chapter reminds me that I have to make a choice. A choice to put God before my husband. A choice to worship God and not a man. This chapter reminds me that though my husband will fail me, my God never will—and that if I'll put my hope in Him, I will never be disappointed.

—Julie

Notes

1. Lee Madden, cited in Chrissy Balz, "Weddings: A Veil of Sadness," *Newsweek*, August 7, 2006.
2. Aviva Patz, "Will Your Marriage Last?" *Psychology Today*, January/February 2000. http://www.psychologytoday.com/articles/pto-20000101-000036.html (accessed May 2007).

CHAPTER 6

A Stalled-Out Relationship

What to Do When Your Husband Won't Change His Irritating Ways

My family was all packed up, ready to head to Telluride, Colorado, for a fabulous ski vacation. The car was loaded with both luggage and kids, and I had just made a final quick bathroom stop. This last stop is essential to remain in good standing with my husband when going on a car trip. You see, he comes from the "vacation starts the minute *you arrive at your desired location*" mentality, so we need to hurry up and get there. No time for excess stopping. I, on the other hand, come from the "vacation starts the minute *you leave the driveway*" mentality, so let's stop often and have fun along the way. But on this particular morning I was interested in being a team player. I wanted vacation harmony (no doubt you know what I mean). So I settled in the car, buckled my seat belt and looked forward to catching up on some meaningful conversations with my husband, who was driving the car.

We hadn't been on the road more than a few minutes when I realized a problem was brewing. The problem? Although I was obviously bending over backward to be thoughtful—no drive-thru Starbucks, no unscheduled potty stop, and so on—*he* didn't seem to be thinking about my needs and feelings at all. He didn't ask if the air conditioner was too cold (it was actually fine). He didn't offer me a look at the map (it was tucked under his sun visor). But worst of all, he didn't ask me what music I wanted to listen to in the car. And here is where the problem really started. It was clear that the only music we were listening to on the 18-hour road trip was *his* music. That might not sound like such a bad thing, but let me offer a little bit of history.

My husband is a die-hard Doobie Brothers fan. Why, he is such a known fanatic that at his 10-year anniversary celebration for pastoring the church we founded, they honored him by having the band play the Doobie Brothers' "Listen to the Music" during the church service! No joke! They honored me by giving us an ornate, engraved tray that was part of my silver pattern (it's quite beautiful). But for Will, a Doobie tune.

Will loves old tunes. Doobie Brothers. Kenny Loggins. Toto. You get the idea. And while I really enjoyed those tunes in the 1980s, I would say that my taste has grown (or rather grown up) as I have matured. I enjoy some contemporary rock. Some folk and blues. A little country. Christian music. Classical. Jazz. But the main point here is that as I have grown, my taste in music has changed—meanwhile as Will has grown, his taste in music has pretty much stayed the same. Not to say I dislike the Doobies and Kenny, but I don't love them enough to listen to them *all the way to Telluride* and that is exactly what was happening.

To get ready for our big car trip, Will had purchased one of those iPod contraptions that hooks up to the car radio. As a result, I was subjected to his '80s oldies for *two whole days* in the car. Now remember my goal was to be a team player, so for the first 400 miles I just tried to talk over the Doobies or sit quietly and listen to Will sing to the Doobies. But when I realized there was absolutely nothing on that iPod besides the '80s music, I just about went out of my mind! He did offer to let me choose one of his CDs, but you must be able to guess what every CD in his holder looked like . . . more '80s music, of course!

I love being married. It's so great to find that one special person you want to annoy for the rest of your life.

—Rita Rudner

I don't know if it was dehydration from trying not to drink and ask for a potty stop or maybe demonic backmasking on those Doobie songs, but at the end of day one, I was a super-sulking mess. I barely talked at all. I was near tears. I felt ignored and alone and misunderstood. And the only thing I kept thinking to myself was, *Will is stuck in the past. He's stalled out. He can't grow and learn to like other music. My husband is musically retarded. This is wrecking our relationship!*

A Stalled-Out Perspective

While some of you might be thinking that I'm being overdramatic, I'll bet many of you can relate. Maybe your husband isn't stuck in the 1980s, but there's probably something he does—or doesn't do—that has threatened to put you over the edge.

Maybe he is stuck in the past because he insists on wearing the same unstylish clothes. You might buy him new clothes and secretly steal Hawaiian shirts out of his closet, but still he won't make the fashion transition. Maybe it's about how he handles the finances—or his lack of handling them.

Or could it be that he seems stalled out spiritually? He sees you reading your Bible and going to Bible study and he, on the other hand, is quite content to sit on the couch and watch TV. He has no desire to go to church at all. Or maybe he's not growing in the area of leading your family. The kids are in need of discipline and guidance, and he's not taking the lead. His absence is leaving a hole of fatherly leadership in your ailing family.

All these situations can lead to friction in the marriage. And while you might have a good attitude or be a team player for a while, at some point it all seems like too much and suddenly you break. You fall into a super-sulk, unable to handle this problem of stunted growth in your husband. He should be growing. He needs to be growing. The lack of growth is killing you and stifling your relationship. And yet, nothing seems to be happening.

So what do you do? You ask him to grow. You plead with him to grow. Finally, you hound him to grow and then there's arguing and dissonance. You're upset. He's livid. And the marriage seems a mess.

Marriage is an alliance entered into by a man who can't sleep with the window shut, and a woman who can't sleep with the window open.
—George Bernard Shaw

But there is hope, my married friend, and it does have to do with growing. It has to do with growing to a new place, a better place, a loving place. *But the growing has to do with you.* Now don't stiffen up—I've got a confession to make first.

Stuck in Selfishness

If you re-read the first several paragraphs of this chapter, you might see something "brewing" between Will and me—something besides the music issue. You might just see that in that particular situation, I made a decision to give to Will, but I was expecting something in return. I planned on going along with Will's "vacation mentality" and I was planning on being a team player, but I also had some great expectations. First, I wanted some reward for being so amiable. I silently expected that Will would attend to my needs and wants. And second, I wanted to be entertained by interesting conversation, while Will was counting on the music to get him through the long drive.

As the hours and miles passed, I remained silent. And I grew more and more angry. I felt mistreated and entitled. My sulking turned into a stew of sympathy—for me! *Poor me,* I said to myself. *Will is not thinking of me. Will is selfishly playing his old music, thinking only of himself. I am sitting here enduring this and thinking only of him. I am quiet and passive, letting him have his way and what good does it do me? I am doing the right thing, while he does the wrong thing and he doesn't even notice.* As I stared out the window watching the scenery speed by, I talked myself right into believing that since I was right—Will must be wrong. And then I started the "What's Wrong with Will List" right there in the car.

Now, of course, you can see that my problem was *me.* Although I was sure I was extremely spiritual and "other-centered," the real truth is, it was all about me. *Me* as the thoughtful one. *Me* as the great sacrificer. *Me* as the sufferer. Me, me, me. *Wah.*

True happiness is knowing you're a hypocrite.

—Ivor Cutler

Okay, let's look at the situation again: Who needs to experience growth? Me or Will? Oh, yes, you see it clearly in my life, but do you see it clearly in yours? Hounding your husband and trying to change him because you perceive he is stalled out is a game for women who feel smug and superior—unable to see their own faults. (I wonder if when Will was driving he was thinking I needed to grow out of my super-sulking mess!)

Starting with Self-Evaluation

In Matthew 7:1-5, there is a telling passage for people who are overly critical. And in this case, let's apply it to wives who harp on and criticize their husbands. Eugene Peterson's *The Message* paraphrases the verses in an eye-opening way. He writes:

> Don't pick on people, jump on their failures, criticize their faults—unless, of course, you want the same treatment. That critical spirit has a way of boomeranging. It's easy to see a smudge on your neighbor's face and be oblivious to the ugly sneer on your own. Do you have the nerve to say, "Let me wash your face for you," when your own face is distorted by contempt? It's this whole traveling road-show mentality all over again, playing a holier-than-thou part instead of just living your part. Wipe that ugly sneer off your own face, and you might be fit to offer a washcloth to your neighbor.

Ouch. But certainly true in my situation.

How about you? Is there a chance that you have criticized your husband unfairly? Are there some areas in your marriage that trigger fault-finding? If so, it can change. Ask God to help you see.

The truth is that I was going crazy because of my own thinking—it really wasn't anything Will was doing at all. The same might be true for you, too. Try to look logically at your situation, and ask God to help you see clearly, to reveal any smug superiority that might be negatively impacting your attitude toward your husband. Stunted growth is quite subjective in many cases and unless it is literally causing you or your children physical or mental harm, it is likely that it's more your problem than your husband's.

If you judge people, you have no time to love them.
—Mother Teresa

So consider moving past your husband's litany of stunted growth, and instead pray for forgiveness for any contempt you might have for him. And you can pray for me, too—that I'll start to love Will more as I "listen to the music."

Loving Your Man

- List three areas of "stunted growth" in your husband. How are these areas driving you crazy? Are these real marital problems or simply irritating personal habits?

- List three areas of "stunted growth" that your husband might identify in your life. How are these areas driving him crazy? Are they real marital problems or simply irritating personal habits?

- Is it easier to see your husband's faults as greater than your own? What is the root of that type of attitude? How is that attitude helping or hindering your relationship with him?

- How often do you pick on your husband? How do you think that critical spirit boomerangs back at you?

- God desires that we treat others as we would like to be treated. Why do you think God made how we treat ourselves the "Golden Rule" standard? What does that say about human nature?

• What are some positive, practical steps you can take to avoid being hypercritical of your husband?

e-Group

"If you can't say anything nice, don't say anything at all." As I read this chapter, the words I heard my mom say hundreds of times echoed in my ears. My mom and Susie are right—nothing good comes from being judgmental or overly critical. And the critical spirit is a tricky one.

I know because there is a critical spirit in our home—it's crept in gradually over the last 20 years. Early in our marriage, the tendency to be critical took the form of mild teasing, like pointing out in a funny way when the other one said or did something silly. Later, the teasing wasn't always so gentle. Then we began to make light of the hurt feelings caused by the unkind words. Finally, the sarcasm snuck in. It's funny in small doses, but not so much when the laughter becomes more important than the other person's feelings.

Recently I realized how critical of each other my husband, Blake, and I had become when I demanded that the kids stop their verbal sparring only to hear in reply, "Why? You and Dad do it all the time." *Touché*. Addressing my son's disrespect was fairly easy. Eliminating the critical spirit has not been, especially when our entire family is suffering from it!

So, if I understand what I've just read, keeping my mouth shut and praying about what I should say and how I should say it is the key. And to think I spent so many years thinking my mom didn't know anything!

—Dee

CHAPTER 7

Romance Redefined

Why Your Marriage Reads Just Like a Romance Novel

Sixty-four million Americans read romance novels every year. And I'm sure it won't surprise you to learn that 78 percent of the readers are women.[1] Apparently readers are so hungry for these dreamy story lines that they shell out over $1 billion annually.[2] Why? Because paying a couple of bucks to get whisked away into a passionate story with an ideal man is a real bargain!

While getting lost in an imaginary love story is entertaining, the truth is that there are many women who'd like a little more romance in their everyday life. Not from a fictionalized Fabio but from the man they married. Women want to feel desired and appreciated—and there's just nothing like a thoughtful gesture from their husband that says, "I love you." It makes women quiver inside to think that they're still special to the man to whom they pledged their life and love. And though it might be normal for married couples to settle into a routine after the wedding, when the routine is void of romance, the reality is quite disappointing.

If things get really crazy, you might find yourself (like a dear friend of mine once did) spending your third wedding anniversary watching your husband play flag football—and then hanging out afterward with his sweaty teammates. It happens. When you throw in a couple jobs and a kid or two, it might seem like there's just no time left for romance. The romance quotient often gets so low that it's as if the relationship is lying still and quite undisturbed—like Sleeping Beauty waiting for a kiss from Prince Charming. How does it happen? Once it was roses, wine and candlelit dinners—now it's diapers, bills and flag football with the guys. It's hard not to get your heart crushed when all you want is a little extra attention, a little wooing—and you can't seem to get it.

Men really do feel incredible passion for their wives,
but they don't recognize it sometimes.[3]
—Dr. Scott Haltzman

With that said, I bet it would surprise you to learn that your husband does indeed desire romance. He wants to woo you. Really! As a matter of fact, 84 percent of men surveyed reported that they desire romance with their wives.[4] Startled? Shocked? I can almost hear the collective gasp as you mutter out loud, "My man must be in the other 16 percent!" But before you write your husband off as nonromantic, let's examine what a romantic man looks like in the first place.

Mr. Romantic?

A romance is a love story. That means that "Mr. Romantic" is a man involved in a love story. A "love story" is a relationship that is marked by expressions of love and affection. While you might be thinking that this definition just proved that your husband is *not* Mr. Romantic—please notice that nowhere in the description is there a mention of roses, wine and candlelight. In other words, a real love story is not defined by gifts or tokens of affection.

A real love story is about *people*. It's about two people com-municating to each other about their ongoing love and commitment. And while there are times when the trinkets are nice, the trinkets are merely symbols of much deeper thoughts and longings. They are tiny glimmers of the reality that lies beneath the surface—*things* meant to speak of an inexpressible love.

Much to the dismay of retailers everywhere, a romantic man is not necessarily the one who comes bearing flowers and chocolates, expensive diamonds, tickets for a Hawaiian getaway or even Hallmark cards. And though I confess that I used to think that external "stuff" defined romance, it definitely does not.

Aren't most romance heroes, or heroes in fiction of any kind, generally superior to real men?
—Nora Roberts

Instead, that is what *culture* has defined as romance. Much like culture has erroneously defined "sexy" as a Victoria Secret bra and thong set (don't get me started), culture has misrepresented what real romance looks like. Think your husband is unromantic if he's not wining and dining you? I have some amazing news: It's simply untrue.

If your husband has yet to send you a massive spray of vibrant roses, that does not mean he's lacking a romance gene. And while I, too, love that kind of fancy, flower-filled thoughtfulness, romance is about something much deeper. Though I do actually consider my husband a romantic at heart, it's not because I've never received an appliance for Valentine's or my birthday! For as much as I delight in the lavish attention associated with all the romantic frills, there is something else I desire more than a new piece of jewelry or an island getaway: *unconditional love in a covenant commitment.* When such love defines a marriage relationship, something unspeakably romantic happens. There is an ongoing communication that unfolds in the relationship—communication I like to refer to as "the tender talk of love." And every relationship that enjoys such tender talk is characterized by a secret, seductive love story, known only to husband and wife. It is something I savor in my own marriage.

The Secret Story of Romance

Now, you might be thinking that Will and I have some sort of fabulously dreamy lifestyle. That we go on numerous dates weekly. That we speak in sonnets and fall asleep tucked in each other's arms. But no, that is not why I believe we have a secret, seductive love story. We're probably just like you and your husband. We both have demanding jobs. We have three kids that still need parenting. We have extended family living literally right down the street. And we spend a lot of time and energy building up the Church. It's really a regular life, but I see us living out a spectacular love story because I understand the unbelievable gift that my marriage to Will really is. And I view the way we communicate our love to each other as extremely romantic.

You don't love someone for their looks, or their clothes, or for their fancy car, but because they sing a song only you can hear.
—Anonymous

See, the truth is that every husband and wife has a special way of communicating their love to each another. And as the marriage blossoms through the years, that communication creates a story. The tender talk in your marriage is a kind of special communication that is more than just words. It's the story of your oneness with your husband. It's an intimacy known through the good times and the bad times. The longer a couple is together, the more the intimacy deepens, with all sorts of nuances known only to the couple. Your marriage becomes much like a romance novel with interesting characters (that would be you and your husband), an appealing setting (right at home where you live) and the tender talk of love between the two of you (a dialogue of sorts) that tells the story.

Right now you may be thinking that I am idealizing your marriage—and that you and your husband are just a regular, ho-hum couple. Or maybe you've even had some excruciating heartache in your marriage, and you really believe that your life is not at all romantic. But let's not use culture's idea of romance as a yardstick to measure by—instead, let's look to what God thinks is romantic.

The Greatest Lover of All Time

God is the ideal romancer because He is the greatest Lover. So how He defines romance is essential for understanding how to gauge life and love—most especially in marriage, one of the most exquisitely beautiful things He created. While mainstream culture dismisses marriage as mundane and outdated, the fact is that a man who is unconditionally devoted to one woman *is* romantic. My friend Liz agrees:

> You know what *real* romance is? A man who comes home every night to his family. A man who provides to the best of his ability for his family. Romance is a man who delights in having sex with his wife of a certain age and body fat. Real romance is through thick and thin. In sickness and in health. You can keep your smooth talkin' men who give good gifts and talk a good game. Give me a man who is steady, reliable, honest and true. That's romance.

I couldn't agree more. To have a man commit "to have and to hold from this day forward, for better or for worse, for richer, for poorer, in sickness and in health, to love and to cherish 'til death do us part" has got to be viewed as one of the great romantic ideas of all time.

The creation of marriage was God's idea, and His ability to take two people and make them one is amazing. Genesis 2:21-24 tells the story from the beginning.

> So the LORD God made him fall into a deep sleep, and he took out one of the man's ribs. Then after closing the man's side, the LORD made a woman out of the rib. The LORD God brought her to the man, and the man exclaimed, "Here is someone like me! She is part of my body, my own flesh and bones. She came from me, a man. So I will name her Woman!" That's why a man will leave his own father and mother. *He marries a woman, and the two of them become like one person* (CEV, emphasis added).

I think this unity between two people in marriage explains the tender love talk enjoyed by couples in a committed, covenant relationship. When two wholly different people come together as one in holy matrimony, it is nothing short of miraculous. And while this reality is expressed sexually, it is also manifested in the routines of day-to-day life. With marriage comes a new way of doing things and thinking things and saying things. It's like there is a whole new way of living and communicating because of the love between a husband and wife—a whole new history is being written. And that tender talk is the expression of romance in marriage.

Your Marital Fingerprint

You see, the way that you and your husband express love to each other is just like a fingerprint—completely individual in every way. Your fingerprint of marriage includes your unique relational history. It includes the love and affection the two of you share.

And it is completely distinctive in expression. The fascinating way you communicate affection is likely often hidden from others but beautifully fulfilling for each of you. And your unique expression of romance—your fingerprint—shapes the whole of your relationship.

Let me illustrate with an example. If I told you that my husband called me a fat pig, you would likely think he was the most insensitive, unbelievably rude man on the planet, and not at all romantic. But that's because you are unaware of our marital fingerprint. The title "fat pig" is actually a deep groove in the fingerprint of our affection for each other.

One particular day on our honeymoon in Maui, Will and I enjoyed a long afternoon at the beach and then came back to the hotel room for the evening. He took a quick shower and relinquished the bathroom to me. When I finished showering and dressing, I opened the bathroom door to find him sprawled out in the middle of the king-sized bed watching, of all things, a Billy Graham crusade on television. When I saw him lying there, eyes fixed on the TV, I said in a most irritated tone, "Move over, you fat pig!" He laughed hysterically as I bounded onto the bed and snuggled up next to him.

Ever since that time, the name has stuck. He is a fat pig. I am a fat pig. It has morphed into "Fatty," "Big Fat Pig," and the list goes on and on. It truly is a term of endearment between the two of us, and we use it all the time. Pretty funny, huh? But what is really funny is the reaction we get in public. Because it's not unusual at all for Will to call out to me at church or a restaurant, "Hey, Fatty, I'm over here." I don't even try to explain to the horrified women who feel sorry for me and cast scornful looks at Will. They just don't understand—and it doesn't matter to me that they don't because that is the unique (somewhat strange) language of love between my husband and me. It is a significant piece of our unique marital fingerprint.

I bet you can relate to that because you have a unique history in your relationship with your husband. There are key phrases and looks and gestures that only the two of you understand. Many times they are simple things—but they mean the world to the two of you.

My friend Debbie told me that if she wants to really say something about how she feels toward her husband, she holds his hand in public. He loves it, and it means much more to him than simply linking hands. Likewise, his tender love talk is changing the sheets on the bed for her after she has had an especially long day at work. They share a unique dialogue only they understand.

My sister Linda says that her husband's "wholehearted acceptance" of who she is as a person—an athlete and nature lover—is romantic. Her husband, Jim, has been known to encourage her to take long romps on the greenbelt behind their house. He even bought her a kayak for her birthday because he understands Linda would rather have a kayak for the creek than a diamond for her finger.

One of the most romantic things Will and I do together is minister. Quite often we teach together at our church services and when we do, our relationship deepens. An inexpressible oneness springs from our teaching God's Word together. While it might be work for some, to stand by his side and proclaim God's truth is one of the richest and most endearing pieces of our relationship.

Finding Your Fingerprint

Every couple's fingerprint is unique, as is their dialogue of tender talk. In order to understand your own, you've got to consider the actions, attitudes and ambience created by the dialogue of love in your marriage. It's the capacity to communicate love in a way that is understood. And at its very core, it's the expression of being known and loved by your spouse. This type of marital intimacy was part of God's original design. When He created marriage, He meant for a husband and wife to have the capacity to commune with complete openness and acceptance. A venerated vulnerability. Genesis 2:25 says it like this: "The man and his wife were both naked, and they felt no shame" (*NIV*). That is a love void of inhibitions—a deeply romantic love.

Your romance is as individual as a fingerprint—filled with mystery and complexity. The daily affections you and your husband share will become more and more apparent as you start to see and understand your secret story. Then you will be flooded with appreciation at being an active partner in a romantic love affair with the man of your dreams. So read your very own romance right there at home, and watch with new eyes as your very own love story unfolds.

Loving Your Man

- How has our culture skewed your view of romance in general and your marriage in particular?

- What is the tender talk of love in your marriage? How do you uniquely love your man? And how does he love you back?

- What experiences have molded your love affair with your husband?

- Identify four different aspects of the fingerprint of your love story that are unfolding in your marriage.

- How is the continual dialogue in your marriage writing a secret, seductive story?

• Why does covenant oneness build the sweetest love story?

e-Group

I do believe in this idea of a fingerprint in marriage, and it's fun to look for it in other couples. There are definitely expressions and gestures Erick and I share that no one outside my marriage would understand. What's so cool to me is that we are all so different and that God uses marriage to fulfill our needs in different ways.

While there have been typical romantic moments in our marriage, many things I consider romantic might not be recognized as such by the general public. God knew what I needed in a mate far better than I could have imagined. He knew that while I love chocolates and flowers, what my soul requires is much more than that. It's romantic to me that I can tell my husband about a situation and that he will call me on it if he thinks my motives aren't totally good (I do the same with him). If I lose a tennis match, he doesn't throw fluffy words all over it; he just puts a big *L* on his forehead with his finger and thumb, and it makes me smile. It's romantic to me that on a Saturday we can go to three of our kids' games, then come home and watch another game on TV as a family, and there is nothing that either of us would rather be doing. And it is very romantic to me that we are good at keeping each other's secrets.

I prayed for my marriage long before I met Erick, and only God knew what I needed. Life has not been perfect, and we have had our share of hard times. But *living* my marriage really is better than *reading* a romance novel, and it's pretty therapeutic to enjoy my very own romance story.

—Jodi

Notes

1. "Reader Statistics," Romance Writers of America, 2007. https://www.rwanation al.org/eweb/dynamicpage.aspx?webcode=StatisticsReader (accessed May 2007).
2. "Romance Statistics," Romance Writers of America, 2002. http://www.storyforu.com/ stats.htm (accessed May 2007).
3. Hara Estroff Marano, "Secrets of Married Men," *Psyched for Success*, July 26, 2004. http://www.psychologytoday.com/articles/pto-20040726-000013.html (accessed May 2007).
4. Shaunti Feldhahn, *For Women Only: What You Need to Know About the Inner Lives of Men* (Sisters, OR: Multnomah Publishers, 2004), p. 139.

Chapter 8

A Failure to Yield

How a Mutually Submitted Relationship Makes Things Run Smoothly

Five years ago, my husband was hit by a car. He was riding his bicycle, going about 25 miles an hour, body tightly tucked to catch speed, when suddenly a car smashed into him. A teenaged driver, anxious to make a left hand turn into Whataburger, failed to yield and literally turned his vehicle right into my husband, catapulting Will and his bike into the air and over the car. Witnesses say that the force was so great that Will flipped twice in the air before his whirling body pummeled into the ground. Few people who saw the accident happen thought Will could have survived. I was at home that morning, and I remember the phone call from the emergency medical technician like it was yesterday.

"Mrs. Davis? Is this Mrs. Davis?" asked the EMT.

"Yes, this is Mrs. Davis," I casually responded.

"Mrs. Davis, I am Linda from Austin Emergency Response. Mrs. Davis, I need you to know that your husband has been hit by a car while cycling. Are you okay, Mrs. Davis?"

"*Will was hit by a car?!*" I shrieked, feeling queasy.

"Yes, Mrs. Davis, but I want you to know that we are taking him to the emergency room right now and I believe he will be fine. Can you meet us there? Is there someone that can drive you to the emergency room to meet us?"

"Yes . . . I will meet you. What happened—is Will really okay? Are you sure Will is okay?"

"Actually, Mrs. Davis, we checked his vital signs, and we have every reason to believe he is going to be okay. But he does need stitches on his hip and . . . oh, just a minute. He would like to talk with you. I am going to hold the phone for him so that he can tell you himself." And then suddenly, Will's voice was on the other end.

"Susie? I'm really going to be okay. They have me in the ambulance, and we're headed to the hospital. I'm going to be alright. Really."

"Oh, my gosh, Will—a car hit you?" I was crying and trying to catch my breath.

"Yes. The driver turned right into me, but I am really going to be okay. Really. Just meet me at the hospital. I'll see you there. Okay?"

As I raced to get my keys, I could only think of a few things. *Breathing. I must keep breathing. And find those stupid keys.* For a moment I saw myself raising our children alone without the man I loved, but it was so overwhelming that I kept myself from thinking about it by concentrating on things like keeping my eyes on the road, making the 20-minute trek to the hospital.

But then a million things flooded my head. *Was Will alright? Were they sure he didn't have internal injuries? When should I tell my children? Who should I call for help?* But mainly, I was just so grateful that I had heard his voice and I had every reason to believe he wasn't critically injured.

When I got to the hospital and rushed inside, I found Will propped up on a pillow, looking pretty scraped up and bloody— but not altogether bad for someone who'd just been hit by a car. I was relieved to finally talk with a doctor and hear that Will's injuries were superficial, only requiring staples to his hip where the asphalt slashed his skin. It was all going to be okay, just like everyone had promised. Within a few hours, Will was rolled out to my car in a wheelchair and we made the drive home.

Right of Way

I think a lot about that kid's failure to yield. How his desire to go first could have seriously messed up so many people's lives. His "me first" mentality could have robbed our family of both husband and father, but it also could have had a terrible impact on his own life. Can you imagine how this young man would have coped with a judgment of involuntary manslaughter? Yikes.

A failure to yield in marriage can create all kinds of problems, too. When we are steadfast in the desire to always think of ourselves first, it's nothing more than a failure to yield. If *our* idea is the *best* idea and *our* plan is the *only* plan, then severe damage in the relationship will certainly be the sad outcome. And just like that teenager's decision to surge ahead caused such trauma, surging ahead when it is time to yield in marriage also creates trauma—the relational kind.

It is God's design that we yield to each other in our relationships. Philippians 2:3-4 tells us, "Do nothing out of selfish ambition or vain conceit, but in humility consider others better than yourselves. Each of you should look not only to your own interests, but also to the interests of others" (*NIV*). God expects us to be willing to yield the right of way, thinking about what is good for other people, not just ourselves.

There are specific guidelines for giving the right of way in marriage. Ephesians 5:21-22 says, "Honor Christ and put others first. A wife should put her husband first, as she does the Lord" (*CEV*). Now, just to let you know, the *New International Version* says it this way: "Submit to one another out of reverence for Christ. Wives, submit to your husbands as to the Lord." Right now you might be thinking, *Submit! I thought you said "yield"—there's a big difference!*

I know how you're feeling. The minute I hear the word "submit," I feel the need to defend myself. And I think this is a typical reaction. As a matter of fact, recently I was exercising and talking with a woman I had just met at the gym, and upon discovering my husband was a pastor, she exclaimed, "Well, I go to church, but I don't submit to my husband." The weird thing is that we hadn't even been talking about submission in marriage.

But her reaction made me realize something: I think at some point along the way the verse has been used by unscrupulous religious people to suppress and deny the dignity of women. At one time that verse was used to make women feel like a doormat in marriage. And so the word "submit" assumed a negative connotation—it was trashed, misused and demonized at the expense of the truth.

Yet if we're honest, we must admit that "submit" means "yield"—same thing—although it certainly does not elicit the same reaction. Look at it this way: If you were pulling onto a busy highway, merging into traffic, and the sign read "Submit" instead of "Yield," would you have a more visceral reaction? I think motorists (men and women alike) would be plowing through that "Submit" sign just to prove that no one is going to make them submit!

When we make a calculated move to surge ahead, failing to yield, we have to realize we will miss the blessing of God's design for our marriage relationship. What you might not realize is that the verse in Ephesians quoted above follows the command to be *mutually* submitted to one another out of reverence for Christ. Mutual submission in marriage means that we each desire to think of the other person's needs before plowing ahead.

Compromise, if not the spice of life, is its solidity. It is what makes nations great and marriages happy.
—Phyllis McGinley

A biblical marriage is yielding to God first, spouse second and self third. Picture a triangle: God is at the top of the triangle,

I am on one of the lower points, and Will is on the other. That makes Will and me equal in our relationship to each other and equal in our access to God. If at any point I blast ahead and place myself above Will, I not only wreck my relational placement with Will biblically, but I also wreck my relational placement with God. If I am steadfastly at the tip-top of the triangle, I have demoted God. When I do that, things get out of whack. God's original intent for a healthy marriage is mutual submission, which creates a balanced, loving and unselfish approach to the marital relationship.

A Wrecked Perspective

Have you ever wondered, *What is it about yielding or submitting that is so unappealing?* For me, the aversion hinges on the possibility that Will might neglect to consider my needs. Or maybe it's because I honestly feel like my idea or plan is better than Will's. I could think of a dozen reasons. But at the root of every reason, there is a deeper explanation, and it's being hung up on the wrong perspective.

When we continue to regard yielding to our husband as the problem, we are blinded to the real issue. It's like this: When I read the Bible and find it filled with all kinds of verses about submitting and yielding and putting others first, it causes me to feel conflicted and tense. And that tension is there because I find it difficult to put myself second to others. By default, I can be a pretty selfish person, so it takes effort and energy for me to be selfless. In reality, the tension I feel when it comes to being others-centered isn't created by other people—it's created by God and what He is asking me to do. See, it's not Will asking me to yield in marriage—it's *God* asking me to yield. So my real frustration surfaces because I have a problem with God and His Word.

Author Anne Lamott wrote something simple and clever that sheds a great deal of light on this issue. She said, "If your wife locks you out of the house, you don't have a problem with your door."[1] Now, obviously, if you locked your husband out of the house, it would be comical for him to insist that the door is the problem. But just for a minute, imagine that he was angry at the door. Maybe he would rail at the door for standing in the way of the relationship. Or perhaps he would involve a specialist in helping him to understand the door better since it was hindering the relationship. That would be pretty absurd, since the real problem in the relationship is the reason why the door was locked in the first place.

But the wisdom that comes from heaven is first of all pure. It is also peace loving, gentle at all times, and willing to yield to others.
James 3:17

Well, the same is true with the command to yield in marriage. Thinking that the idea of submission is the problem is just as ludicrous as thinking that the door is the problem. My irritation about yielding to Will isn't really about Will at all; it's about yielding to what God asks of me. The sooner I understand the real issue, the better, because that will help me to do something about the problem. I need to remember that what God asks me to do is for my own good and the good of the relationships in my life. God knows that when I follow His way of doing things, my life and my marriage will be blessed. And though that may sound very simple, living it out is far more complex.

The Risky Reality of Yielding

What I didn't tell you at the beginning of the chapter is that after Will's accident, I *did not* want him to ride again. As a matter of fact, I felt it was irresponsible of him to get back on a bike and risk dying—leaving me a widow and our children fatherless. But I also knew something else. I knew that Will was an avid cyclist, that he absolutely loved cycling, that it was one of his favorite leisure activities. So when we were on our way back from the hospital and the subject of cycling came up, I had to pray for the grace to respond in a loving and wise way. I prayed to yield to God about this cycling issue, knowing that how I treated Will in this situation would ultimately reflect upon me and my relationship with God. So I prayed. And I secretly hoped that Will wouldn't want to cycle—that the accident had dampened his desire.

I was dead wrong. On the way home, Will told me that he still wanted to ride. That he couldn't imagine not riding. After he finished talking, I told him what I felt (without hysterics) and asked him to pray about God's will concerning his cycling habit. He promised he would pray about it.

One month later, Will went out and purchased a brand-new road bike. I didn't say a word and I didn't get angry—but I prayed like mad. Within three rides, Will was ready to hang up the bike. He simply lost the desire. As avid as he was about cycling, he discontinued riding.

When I look back on that time, I am amazed at how God enabled me to yield to Will. While I was terrified at the thought of Will riding again, God reminded me that *He* was in control. He infused me with strength to submit to Will's decision, even though I didn't like it. I was able to lean into God for Will's protection—since *He* is the only One really able to protect Will anyway. I trusted God to work out the problem. And instead of barging ahead with *my way*, I was able to yield and avoid relational wreckage.

Things don't always work out that way, of course—all wrapped up in a bow. As a matter of fact, as I wrote this chapter I was sitting in the car, trying to learn (all over again) to yield, as

Will drove the family to Waco to see our college-aged son. And I was a wreck. You see, two years ago I was in a horrible head-on accident and, as a result, I have some "driving baggage." So as I was sitting in the passenger seat, typing away on my computer with the iPod buds in my ears, I heaved sighs every time Will hit a certain speed. I sporadically pressed my foot on the floorboard, using my imaginary brake when I thought he was tailing someone too closely. My great wish? For him to slow down to granny-speed and turn down those blasted '80s tunes. I wanted him to take this driving thing more seriously!

But lurking in the back of my mind was the understanding that at that moment I was struggling to trust God with my family and to yield to others. My maniacal raging in the car at that moment would not help or change Will's driving, nor would it model to my girls what it looks like to love and respect a man. I really didn't want to be the weirdo wife driving the family, husband in the passenger seat, because she didn't trust her husband to do a good job. And so I cried out on the inside for God to help as I struggled. And I tried with everything inside me to act like the person I want to be—a wife that is willing to yield to the greater good: my husband and my family.

What I realize more and more through these situations is that fighting to get my way is really about me and my lack of trust in God to take care of the big picture. It's about my screaming at the locked door instead of crying out to God. And though I think I'd like to micromanage the lives of my loved ones, it's only because I erroneously think I know best. But the ongoing truth is that *God knows best*. He knows best about the little things and the big things—and the one thing He has assigned me to manage is how I treat people in the process. While learning to yield in relationships takes perspective and practice, ultimately it's about yielding the right of way simply because that's what God says is right.

Loving Your Man

- How do you feel about the word "submit"? Is "yield" an easier word to accept? What do you think has created your distaste for "submission"?

- In a healthy marriage, what does mutual yielding look like? (For example, what does mutual yielding look like when it comes to financial decisions? Or childrearing issues?)

- Why are the root issues important to consider as you seek to understand your resistance to yielding?

- List five areas in which your husband has yielded to you. List five ways you have yielded to your husband.

- What is the one area in your marriage that creates the most tension because of a lack of mutual submission? Is there some action you could take to honor God further, and thus lesson the tension?

- Is there a situation in which it would be biblical not to submit? What guidelines should be considered to ensure that God is honored?

- Should a Christian wife yield to a non-Christian husband? Are there ways she could yield while maintaining her spiritual dignity?

e-Group

I feel like I am always yielding to my husband's desire. I feel like I am always the one "giving in." Oh, sure, I might nag and moan, but by golly, he ends up getting his way. Which means I'm yielding, right?

I really didn't think I had an "issue" with submission—until I read Susie's chapter. Then I actually felt annoyed because not only am I not yielding to Steve, I am also not yielding to God! I didn't like that idea, so I put the chapter down and stopped reading. But it kept beckoning me. And in the back of my mind, I knew there was something to it, so I kept chewing on the idea that struggling with submission is really about my relationship with God.

The truth is, this chapter made me look squarely in the face of my "moaning and groaning" submission and recognize the fact that it isn't submission at all. The chapter helped me to see that giving in doesn't make me a good wife or a good Christian. I actually need to humbly submit my will before God, not Steve.

—Liz

Note

1. Anne Lamott, *Bird by Bird* (New York: Anchor Books, 1994), p. 178.

Fatal Detraction

Recently, Will and I were looking through some pictures from our wedding and honeymoon (circa 1985). I have to tell you, I was startled by several things. For one, there was a lot of '80s "poof" going on. Will had a full head of thick brown hair—it's now buzzed à la Lance Armstrong—and I had some seriously highlighted, rolled blonde poof. My bridesmaids wore billowing, bubblegum-pink taffeta dresses with big poofy sleeves. (What was I thinking?) We had peonies everywhere at the ceremony. They were fragrant and beautiful, but also quite poofy. And my sister, who served as matron of honor, was, well, poofy. She was *over* nine months pregnant at the time of our wedding—which means she was extremely poofy. Yes, everything was '80s "poof" except our lean 20-something bodies. Those were anything but poofy.

Then as I was flipping through the photos of our honeymoon, I just couldn't help but think back and sigh a little sigh. Looking at all those pictures of us on our honeymoon was somewhat bittersweet. There we were in our bathing suits, kissing under a secluded Hawaiian waterfall. And there we were again in our bathing suits, waving to the camera while parasailing. And again, in our bathing suits, eating breakfast on the balcony of our suite. Didn't we wear anything else on our honeymoon?! Well, I guess I shouldn't answer that.

It would have been great if the honeymoon could have lasted a little longer. The impatient desire, the spontaneity and, of course, the youthfulness! Oh, I know there are seasons for everything and I don't expect to live out married life on Honeymoon Island, but I do want certain things for my marriage—and yours.

I long for wives to desire their husbands. And I would like for us, as wives, to think more about the physical aspects of pleasing our husbands. I want us as women to battle against the idea that a "regular, ho-hum routine" is all we need to have after the honeymoon. Don't get me wrong; I'm not talking about a feverish, out-of-control affair with your husband, but I do think it's healthy to experience some serious mutual attraction. Why? Because a relationship devoid of attraction can create a stalemate in a marriage. So let's get busy defeating those negative thoughts and habits that keep you from enjoying your husband.

CHAPTER 9

He's Hot to Someone

How an Attitude Adjustment Could Save Your Marriage

My 40-something friend Dee had a problem, and she didn't know it. But I would not let her suffer because I care about her and her marriage to Blake, her husband.

Blake is a barefoot water skier. And he's really good. He's so good, in fact, that he competed in a national competition and got his photo plastered across the front page of the paper. Not a big deal, except he was performing a tumble turn, his able body skimming across the surface of the water, and looking like a 20-year-old.

Now, here is the potential problem. Let's say Dee wakes up and has no idea Blake (and his tan, muscular body) is laid out in the newspaper. Like any other normal wife, she wakes up, throws her hair in a ponytail and puts on her grubby carpool clothes. She takes care of the children's breakfast, makes their lunch and loves on the "baby," their pug puppy. Then she hurries the kids out the door. Let's say she does manage a quick "goodbye" and a peck on the cheek for Blake as she leaves. Then he gathers his things and heads out the door to work. They won't see each other again for a good eight hours. And after eight hours, she'll probably be wiped out from carting the kids to their various after-school functions. She might be dragging around trying to get dinner on the table, help the kid's finish their homework, listen to their stories about school peer pressure, and she might even wonder out loud why Blake didn't get the trash can to the curb. Oh, yeah, Blake. Almost forgot about him—you know, the man of her dreams, her husband.

But before this imaginary situation could ever start to materialize, enter Susie, Dee's dear friend. Knowing the above is very typical in any American home, I called Dee early in the morning, right after I saw the photo of Blake in the paper. I called but I didn't let her know it was me.

The phone rings. Dee answers.

"Hello?"

I disguise my voice completely, attempting to sound young and eager.

"Hi! Um, I was wondering if I could talk with Blake?"

Dee sounds curious, "Could I ask who is calling?"

I giggle in a girlish way, "Oh, well, I just saw Blake's picture in the paper skiing, and I just wanted to tell him that he looks hot! It's just so cool he can do that barefoot stuff. Wow! Do you think I could talk to him?"

Dee, on the offensive, "Well, this is his wife. I could tell him for you, okay?!"

I laugh now, unable to help myself. She's relieved it's me and is somewhat annoyed I am so juvenile.

But after spoofing her on the phone, I told her to watch her back. I recognized that Blake looked good (okay, great!) in the paper, and I told her that I was her "warning." We had a good laugh over it (and so did Blake).

But the truth be told, we all need the warning.

Wake Up and Smell the Coffee

Our husbands might as well be in the paper looking really good every day. Think about it. They are around other women all day who are likely to notice their good looks, good manners and good hearts. They're out in the world, cleaned up and smelling good—looking like a real catch for some man-hungry woman.

It's pretty easy to get into a daily grind of housework and homework and forget about that appealing man you married. It's easy to allow irritations and incidentals to distract you. But the one important thing to remember (and this is vital) is: That man you married is hot to someone. And the truth be told, it would be best if you let him know that he is hot to you!

I'm not quite sure exactly how or why we take each other for granted, no longer manifesting that "hot honeymoon" mindset, but give any couple a year or two of marriage and the day-to-day routines of life begin to act like a bucket of cold water on their once-smoldering attraction. Toss in a couple of kids, a job or two, a mortgage and some in-laws and a wife might wonder what in the world she ever saw in her husband that brought them together. Those everyday circumstances seem to make a wife unable to think of her husband as a hottie. But married life doesn't have to be that way.

Hang with me here as the Bible leads us to a piece of practical advice—a way to keep the attraction for that man of yours going strong . . .

In 1 Thessalonians 5:18, the Bible tells us, "Give thanks in all circumstances, for this is God's will for you in Christ Jesus" (*NIV*). Giving thanks in all circumstances includes the ongoing situations of everyday life—the day-in and day-out living with the people in your life. And in particular, the man you chose to marry. In all those aspects of marriage—working, child rearing, good health and bad, taxes, extended family and the like—give thanks with your husband in mind.

In nine cases out of ten, a woman had better
show more affection than she feels.
—Aristotle

Are you looking into the eyes of a man who seems distracted by work and responsibility? Give thanks for his job and his
ability to work hard for your family.

Irritated and baffled by his inability to get his dirty clothes
in the hamper? Give thanks for the fact that he has worked to
provide clothes for his family.

Upset about the lack of help with the kids? How about thank-
ing God for the fact that you have a man to raise the kids with?

Tired and annoyed that he wants to watch ESPN on TV at
night? Well, he is a man, you know, and *aren't you glad you have one?*

Feeling Blessed with the Best

I know that it might seem simplistic to give thanks as a way to
draw you to your husband—but I have found it to be true. Why,
just writing this makes me feel blessed to have Will's attention
and commitment. Thinking about the good things instead of
the bad things makes life sweet, and giving thanks for the many
things in your marriage that you now take for granted is the
way to see your husband through new eyes.

*Recent studies have shown that focusing on the good
things in life actually makes you feel better. Robert Emmons,
a leading gratitude researcher at the University of California
at Davis, reports that expressing gratitude makes people
"feel better about themselves, have more
energy and feel more alert."*[1]

During a particularly glum season in my marriage, I started
a "gratitude" journal. Every morning I listed things for which
I was grateful. It started fairly generic and got more detailed as I
went along. As days turned into months, my ability to see with

eyes of thankfulness became more astute. And as the months rolled into a year, I found myself at an entirely new place of awareness. I had heeded the words of Colossians 3:15, a verse that tells us to cultivate thankfulness.

"Cultivating" is about tending something so that it will grow. So why not apply that scriptural principle of cultivating gratitude to how you view your husband?

The truth is, there is nothing in your life right now (including your husband) that could not be regarded as a gift from God. Your husband is a gift and he, by God's grace, is *your gift alone.* Now why not start giving God thanks by appreciating what you've got? Peel off those ungrateful lenses and see what you have—manifest an attitude of gratitude and thanks for the man who has committed his life to you.

Does he still look good in a pair of jeans? Does he make you laugh like no one else? Is he distinguished looking? Is he cute and manly when he's all hot and bothered when he's working in the garage? (It's even better if *you* get hot and bothered watching him when he's working in the garage!) Then tell him you're attracted to him! Or better yet, show him. But whatever you do—acknowledge and appreciate that he's hot—*to you.*

Definitely a Dreamboat

I have a friend we could all learn from when it comes to appreciation. Liz has been married to Steve for 18 years. About a month ago, I opened my email and read that Liz wouldn't be coming to our monthly Bunko game. I wasn't surprised. She was going on her third week of taking care of her two school-aged children by herself because Steve was working out of town. I expected that she would be wiped out from working a full-time job, managing the household and attending to the kids by herself. Steve was also expected back in town, and I knew she would likely want to see him before he left again on his next business trip. None of this took me off guard—no. However, in the text of the email, there was something that startled me.

> It looks like I won't be there. I'm sorry! The Dreamboat will be back in town and I want to hang out with the fam. xoxoxoxo —liz

What startled me was the fact that she referred to Steve as "the Dreamboat." Honestly, for her to refer to him like this was not new to me, but it did make me chuckle. I knew that as much as she loves her husband and as dreamy as he likely is, he couldn't possibly *always* meet the "dreamboat" criteria.

Dreamboat. You know that man who always does the right thing and says the right thing—and always looks great. He always anticipates a woman's every need, knows her ever-changing moods and is unmoved no matter the circumstances. Dreamboat. A man who's easy to live with, never gets on your nerves and never exasperates or challenges your expectations. Dreamboat. Romantic yet realistic. Strong yet sensitive. Virile but always the gentleman. A man to love with all your heart and all your mind. *Whew.*

Why, the extended travel alone would certainly disqualify Steve from many weary wives' Dreamboat List. But there was my friend Liz, insistently referring to "the Dreamboat."

I brought up this apparent fictionalization to Liz the next day when we talked on the phone. And do you know what she said? "It's all in the marketing, honey! If I call him the Dreamboat long enough, he'll be just the Dreamboat I need."

Marketing Your Man in Your Mind

I thought a lot about that after I hung up, wondering if it really is all in the marketing. Marketing, as you know, is all about promoting, selling and distributing a product or service. And in this case marketing means that you actively promote your husband as *the* man of your dreams. The marketing becomes effective when you buy in to the fact that your husband is your dreamboat—your man of everlasting attraction. That buy-in will impact your actions and thoughts.

So follow Liz's lead. She is vitally aware of the importance of her attitudes, thoughts, actions and words regarding her husband. Somewhere, some time, she grabbed on to the idea, and for as long as I have know her, she has been about the business of promoting Steve as "the Dreamboat." What we are busy promoting is what we are likely to believe. As she continually projects her dreamboat image onto Steve—she is consistently conforming him to that image in her mind. He is the man of attraction where she is concerned, and she shows it.

Now, let me be honest. I lunch with Liz monthly (and have for years), and that's long enough to know that Steve and Liz have had their share of the typical marital ups and downs. They have experienced job uncertainty, familial illness, moves and the ongoing challenges of finances, extended family and friends. Oh, yes—they are just like me and you—they have seen it all when it comes to trials in marriage. But in all these things, Steve is still "the Dreamboat." And I think there is a reason for that: Liz tenaciously hangs on to the idea of being grateful for what she has in Steve. In addition, she's smart enough to realize that though Steve is *not* perfect (and she would be quick to say neither is she), he *is* the man of her dreams. Good and bad times, he is the one who is there. He's "the Dreamboat."

That's gratitude, and it works. You might want to test out this whole gratitude/attraction connection. Better you than some young chick at your husband's office. Because just remember, that man of yours is hot to someone, and your marriage will be much happier if he is hot to you!

Loving Your Man

- When was the last time you thought of your husband as a "hottie"?

- Think back to your initial attraction to your husband. What were the physical qualities that made your heart pound? What were the internal qualities that were especially attractive?

- List at least five qualities that attract you to your man. (For example, sporty, intelligent, hardworking, helpful, funny, fit, spiritual.)

- What circumstances cause you to overlook the fact that you're married to an amazing man (not just a financial provider, roommate or lawn-mowing service)? How might gratitude help you guard against taking your man for granted?

- How will you cultivate gratitude in your marriage?

- Who has your back where your marriage is concerned? Would you be willing to enlist a friend to encourage you to love your husband more? (Be sure to invite a friend who also desires a strong marriage of her own— and make sure your friend is female.)

- Try a little experiment: This week, keep a gratitude journal and see how many times you can compliment and/or think well of your husband. Then grade your "attitude of gratitude."

e-Group

Every wife needs this wake-up call. I had one loud and clear about a year ago when my husband's old college girlfriend began calling his office. She called to tell him she would occasionally be coming to town on business and wanted to see if they could get together.

Although Erick didn't agree to meet with her and she lived 2,000 miles away, I was a green-eyed, monstrous wreck. I lost sleep. I Googled her. I even printed out pictures of our happy family to send her. All it took was a simple but very frank phone call from my husband to end her pursuit. But the reality is that it easily could have been a different season in our marriage, and a phone call from an old girlfriend could have been just what my husband thought he needed.

I love that this is an honest, practical chapter encouraging passion and pursuit from the wife for a change. The gratitude journal is a great idea because thinking about the things I am grateful for in my husband really does make him more irresistible to me. A thankful heart, a passionate marriage, an emotionally satisfied man. Sounds like a win-win situation for both of us. Sign me up.

—Jodi

Note

1. Lauren Aaronson, "Make a Gratitude Adjustment," *Psychology Today*, March/April 2006. http://www.psychologytoday.com/articles/pto-20060227-000004.html (accessed May 2007).

CHAPTER 10

Let It Rain

Why Sex to a Man Is Like Rain in a Drought

Rain. We haven't seen any in Austin in 67 days. That might not seem like a big deal if you're sitting at a Starbucks sipping coffee in Seattle, but here in Texas, a lack of rain can be a real problem. In my neighborhood alone, once-lush green yards are now parcels of matted dry tundra, crispy and brown. The magnificent Live Oaks sit stressed, pining away in the summer sun.

But that's not the only thing—even more serious is the plight of ranchers and farmers statewide. They are feeling the financial squeeze of one of the longest running droughts in Texas. It's so severe that many ranchers are forced to sell off cattle, unable to feed them due to the deterioration of pastureland and the rising cost of coastal hay. Farmers, watching crops dry up and wither away, are losing their livelihood. And we, the consumers, are feeling the ripple effect at the grocery store.

While we often don't think of it in these terms, a drought truly is a natural disaster. It isn't as quick and dramatic as a flood, and it certainly lacks the panache of a tornado, but it brings with it costly and devastating effects that are felt by many.

Forecasting a Relational Disaster

While a lack of necessary rainfall creates a drought that is a *natural* disaster, a lack of sex in marriage creates a drought that is a *relational* disaster. Just as the lack of rainfall creates an imbalance in the unseen water table deep within the earth, a lack of sex in marriage creates an imbalance in the unseen parts of a man's psyche deep within his heart. A marriage absent of regular, enthusiastic sex is bound to have a drought-like effect in the relationship. Slowly but surely, the landscape of a marriage dries and fades, until all that is left are the mechanics of two people living together without any enriching sexual dynamic. The ripple effect can be long lasting and far-reaching for any married couple—paralyzing the potential for physical attraction. And while it might not seem like a big deal that it hasn't "rained" in a while, the truth is that refraining from sex in marriage is a set-up for a relational disaster of epic proportions.

Sex is good for a man's physical health as well as emotional health. Studies show men who have sex three or more times a week have a fifty percent reduced risk of heart attack or stroke.[1]

There is a reason that a lack of sex creates relational disaster in marriage, and it has to do with how your man feels about sex. Most women agree that men desire a lot of sex, but we are often completely uninformed about the reasons why. Our culture would like us to think they are testosterone-laden cads or, even worse, perverts that just can't get enough. But the truth is we can't really come close to understanding the deep psychological need men have for sex in marriage nor how it fulfills them. Shaunti Feldhahn, author of *For Women Only: What You Need to Know About the Inner Lives of Men*, surveyed hundreds of husbands regarding their feelings about sex (and lack of sex) in marriage. After reading through thousands of surveys, she concluded this:

For your husband, sex is more than just a physical act. Lack of sex is as emotionally serious to him as say, his sudden silence would be to you, were he simply to stop communicating with you. It would be just as wounding to him, just as much a legitimate grievance—and just as dangerous to your marriage.[2]

Sexual intimacy for a man is the nourishment that deeply waters his male psyche. When he is rejected or ignored when it comes to sexual intimacy, it is as if he is dehydrated—drained dry of one of the most enjoyable aspects of his marriage. For a husband, sex is a vulnerable, amazing act, and abstaining from it—either from an unwilling or unenthusiastic wife—is one of the most depressing things he will endure. If you think I'm overstating it, and you're really brave, just ask your husband how he feels about it.

Seventy percent of men think about sex every day— that's double the rate among women. Statistically, 43 percent of men think about sex several times a day; just 13 percent of women do that.[3]

God's Idea of Dual Ownership

For a typical woman, sex is a pleasurable, fulfilling part of marriage. Enjoying a healthy sex life with her husband provides a deep connection that she shares with no other. And while the act of sex is nearly inexpressible for a woman, it completely defies description for a man. Sex, for a man, is like his lifeline. It is the one place to find complete acceptance, solace and empowerment as a man.

I believe that is why the Bible addresses the issue of sex in marriage. God understands our human makeup and what it takes to maintain our wellbeing. He also cares about what keeps our relationships healthy. Because of that, He gives guidelines when there might be room for debate or difference of opinion. Check out 1 Corinthians 7:3: "The husband should not deprive his wife of sexual intimacy, which is her right as a married woman, nor should the wife deprive her husband." This verse goes so far as to state that sex in marriage is a *right*, as in something to which someone is entitled. Which is likely why 1 Corinthians 7:3 is followed by verse 4, which reads, "The wife gives authority over her body to her husband, and the husband also gives authority over his body to his wife." The biblical picture of sex in marriage equals dual ownership. He willingly gives his body to you, and you in turn willing give your body to him.

To give yourself over to another person, passionately and nakedly, to adore that person body, soul, and spirit—we know there is something special, even sacramental about sex.[4]

Maybe when you read the above verses and consider the concept of ownership, you picture yourself never having an option where sex is concerned. You think that if you never "deprive" your husband of sex and always give your body over to him—you will be having sex *all the time*! Rain, rain, rain—and never a drop of sunshine. But that's not true, and deep down inside I think we all know that. Right now, you may be thinking that I don't understand the height of your husband's sex drive . . . and of course I don't. But I do know this—men have other interests and desires besides sex. They eat and drink and work and exercise.

They read and watch TV and do chores around the house. You know, there are only 24 hours in a day, so there's only so much energy to give to sex anyhow.

But I do think the root issue here is that so many married women worry that if they "give in" and have sex "whenever" their husbands want it—they'll become sex slaves, chained to the whim of their sex-crazed husbands. And that is the thinking that can bring about the drought in the relationship.

Look at it this way: It's human nature to get more insanely desirous of the thing you think you can't have. If you love, love, love chocolate, and then I mandate that you can only have chocolate when I feel like giving it to you, you will not only want the chocolate more but you'll also grow to resent me for keeping it from you when you want it. The same with sex. If your husband desires sex with you and you keep it from him, he will just keep wanting it more and resenting you for keeping it from him. I think that's the reason God gives us this mandate in the Bible in the first place—He understands human nature. He also understands a man's deep need for sexual intimacy in marriage. And He is giving us guidelines to ensure that there isn't a drought in our marital relationship.

The Mystery of Desire

So if you're willing to accept that sex is a big deal to your husband and you're ready to yield to God's guidelines when it comes to sex in marriage, the question becomes, *How do you grow to become a sexually satisfying wife in your marriage?* Because it's likely that you aren't trying to deny your husband—quite the contrary—but you just don't completely understand your husband's needs. And often it is difficult to know how to measure that unseen "water table" deep in your husband's male psyche, making sure it isn't dangerously low. So how do you "rain" consistently, willingly and adequately to ensure the relationship stays healthy?

For most women I know, the issue of sexual desire is fairly complex and mysterious. It's not as if they don't like sex—it's just that the desire doesn't pop up on the radar screen as often as it does for their husbands. While some of that might have to do with waning hormone levels, I think the bulk of it has to do with something far more commonplace.

While reading the book of Song of Solomon (a lover's story), I found a little verse that adequately describes the sometimes mysterious reason women aren't as apt to act on sexual desire as often as men. The context of the following verse is a portion of some serious wooing between Solomon and his "beloved." As a matter of fact, the entire chapter is a building crescendo to the climax of longing.

What startled me in particular was the fact that right in the middle of all this verbal foreplay is a quick, impulsive line expressed by the woman: "Quick! Catch all the little foxes before they ruin the vineyard of your love, for the grapevines are all in blossom" (2:15). Apparently, right there in the midst of this "moment," the woman realizes the potential for a major distraction. And it is so overwhelming to her that she senses if Solomon's not able to jump in and do something about it, it might just ruin the blossoming of their tryst. The reference is metaphorical, of course. There are no real furry foxes running through a vineyard eating the grapes. Instead, what she's saying is, "Quick! Kiss me! Take me—before this building sexual desire dies on the vine." It's the distraction—that's the thing.

Draining Distractions

Can you relate? Aren't there times when you think about sex and get in the mood, then within two seconds you are fully transfixed on something far, far away from sex? It's like my new kitten, Madeleine. She is extremely affectionate and she can be meowing away, sashaying right into my arms—and then in a moment she can be distracted by a sound or a sight and she's gone. I am left standing calling for her, and she's already far away, held captive by the distraction.

I bet the same is true for you. You see your husband, and he looks cute and manly and you think, *I married the cutest guy. Yum, I want to kiss him and hold him.* And then something happens. In a flash, in come the "foxes." Maybe your daughter walks in to talk with you, crying because she had a horrible day at school. Or maybe all of a sudden you feel the love handle sitting stupidly at your waist, and you feel fat and unattractive. Or out of the blue something on your to-do list pops up before your eyes. Or per-haps you're even turned off because you unexpectedly see the trash filled to overflowing, and you realize that really cute guy you married forgot to take out the trash—again! It's like snap, boom! . . . and the moment is gone. All that blossoming love has been sucked right out of you. The sensual feelings vanish—and mundane reality marches in and slams the garden gate shut.

Have you ever wondered at your capacity to turn off your sexual desire so quickly? If you haven't, no doubt your husband certainly has marveled at your ability to go from hot to cold in a matter of minutes. Those foxes that steal from the vine are the very forces that spoil the passion when it comes to sexual enjoyment—and marital bliss.

Outfoxing the Cycle

To fully understand the foxes of distraction, let's go back to our weather analogy of rain one more time. When it rains outside, you probably don't put a lot of thought into remembering what you learned in grade school about the rain cycle. But if you think back, you might recall that in order for rain to drop from the clouds, several things have to happen. There's got to be some

evaporation and condensation, and then finally you get precip-
itation or rain. And while that sounds like a pretty simple cycle,
it's actually extremely complex. Meteorologists would tell you
that beyond the mechanics of rainfall, there are the global
weather patterns that affect jet stream activity, which ultimately creates those heavy, rain-filled clouds. In other words, a lot of
factors have to be *just right* before any rain will actually fall. As a
matter of fact, when we finally do see that rain falling from the
sky, about a million things went on *before* the rain actually fell
from the sky.

Ditto for a woman's desire for sex. Like the rain cycle, women
are complex. And often the desire for sex is somewhat unpre-
dictable—like the weather. Many times it's as if conditions need
to be perfect in order to create the right climate for sexual desire.
Now while that is completely understandable, life doesn't often
present the perfect, fox-free climate. So while there are usually
foxes aplenty, there are many times when a woman should ignore
the need for the perfect conditions and just rain anyway. If she is
married to a man who is desperately thirsty, his water table waning fearfully low, it's actually her responsibility.

But how? How does a woman work at giving exactly what
her husband needs when it is not always what she wants? By
loving him. And consistently putting his needs before everything else that might be distracting her. By creating a lifestyle
of attentive, unwavering physical love. It's exactly the kind of
love a mother exemplifies for her children. If your little one
came to you crying, desperate for attention, could you turn
your back on the need? Not likely—you would drop what you
were doing and comfort and care for the child with loving
words and an embrace. The same is true for our husbands—
but even more so. Though they don't come to us crying for
sex with their words, they have an unspoken need to be physically loved—and it is our responsibility as wives to stop what

we are doing, put away the distractions and rain down our love on them.

Don't let the foxes rob the love and the life from your marriage. Chase them out, and fulfill your role as the one person designed and ordained by God to meet your husband's needs. Love on him with your heart and your body—giving him ownership of the one thing he desperately needs and cannot get anywhere else in his life—*you*.

Loving Your Man

- What are your feelings regarding the concept that a sexless marriage creates relational disaster? Are there some situations in which a sexless marriage is acceptable?

- How important do you think sex is for your husband? Do you think he is able to honestly talk about his sexual needs with you? Why or why not?

- If you were able to gauge your husband's unseen water table, how full would you guess it is?

- While all men are different, what are some signs that your husband's water table is low? What are the factors in his life that create a real drain on his internal reservoir?

- How do you feel about 1 Corinthians 7:3-4? Discuss what "rights" to sexual intimacy look like in a healthy marriage. What about in an unhealthy marriage? How do you feel about the biblical concept of "dual ownership"?

- List 10 foxes that steal from the vineyard of sexual desire.

- How complex and mysterious is your capacity for sexual desire? Do you understand the things that help and hinder your sex drive? What would you be willing to do to adjust your life to "rain down" on your husband more often?

e-Group

I have to admit—this chapter completely annoyed me, but not for the reasons you might think. It annoyed me because for the six months leading up to my marriage, I felt like all I heard from my friends (who were already married) were tips on how to "get through" sex. I have to say that as a 28-year-old virgin, it was completely disheartening! I had been waiting *all this time*, and now everyone was making it sound like sex was something that I wasn't even going to like. However, I held fast to my hope that intimacy with my husband would be something precious and sweet. I was not disappointed.

Now I know what you're thinking, *She's just a newlywed. Give her time; she'll change her tune.* I sincerely hope not. I hope that I'll always remember what this chapter said—that sex makes my husband feel loved and connected and treasured. I hope I'll also remember something that I've discovered: Sex is not just fun and enjoyable; it's also a place where I feel loved and accepted. It may sound crazy, but it is the moment in my day when I feel most beautiful. Why? Because in that moment, I see myself through my husband's eyes instead of the world's. It is one of the sweetest parts of my marriage. And not because we are newlyweds and we're having sex all the time (on the contrary, we work at very demanding jobs, spend many hours serving at our church and often collapse into bed exhausted at the end of the day).

It is sweet because in sex, I have discovered the unrivaled joy that comes from fulfilling the needs of the one I love most and, in doing so, finding myself fulfilled, too.

—Julie

Notes

1. Gail Sheehy, "Why Marriage Is Good Medicine for Men," *Parade Magazine*, June 18, 2006, p. 5.
2. Shaunti Feldhahn, *For Women Only: What You Need to Know About the Inner Lives of Men* (Sisters, OR: Multnomah Publishers, 2004), p. 92.
3. Gary Langer with Cheryl Arnedt and Dalia Sussman, "Primetime Live Poll: American Sex Survey," October 21, 2004. http://abcnews.go.com/Primetime/News/story?id=156921&page=1 (accessed May 2007).
4. John Eldredge, *The Journey of Desire* (Nashville, TN: Thomas Nelson, 2000), p. 134.

CHAPTER 11

Languishing Lovers

When an Uninspiring Marriage Might Signal
a Needed Career Change

Forbes.com did something really brave. They published an article by editor Michael Noer about the negative aspects of a two-career marriage. Mr. Noer made an aggressive assertion in an online article that if men want to be happy, they shouldn't marry career women. If you dare, read on:

> Guys: a word of advice. Marry pretty women or ugly ones. Short ones or tall ones. Blondes or brunettes. Just, whatever you do, don't marry a woman with a career. Why? Because if many social scientists are to be believed, you run a higher risk of having a rocky marriage. While everyone knows that marriage can be stressful, recent studies have found professional women are more likely to get divorced, more likely to cheat and less likely to have children. And if they do have kids, they are more likely to be unhappy about it. A recent study in *Social Forces*, a research journal, found that women—even those with a "feminist" outlook—are happier when their husband is the primary breadwinner. Not a happy conclusion, especially given that many men, particularly successful men, are attracted to women with similar goals and aspirations. And why not? After all, your typical career girl is well educated, ambitious, informed and

engaged. All seemingly good things, right? Sure . . . at least until you get married. Then, to put it bluntly, the more successful she is, the more likely she is to grow dissatisfied with you.[1]

Now, while I am not about to touch his comments or the study itself, that last line about the wife growing dissatisfied sparked my interest. And it's the part that bothered me the most, because dual career or not, I think many wives struggle with growing dissatisfied with their husbands. Why, just last week I was at a neighborhood event, and I overheard two women discussing the fact that they didn't know if they "really loved" their husbands anymore. It seems love grows cold—or wives get bored or distracted—and many lose the passionate affection that they once felt for their husbands. And while I honestly don't buy the whole idea that professional women are more likely to be less satisfied in their marriages, I do think that there is some truth in the idea that a career can get in the way of loving a man—but so can the kids and the house and a whacked-out schedule.

Courting a New Career

There are so many different things vying for my attention as a woman, and I believe any and all of them can cause my love for my husband to languish. If I allow those things to sap my energy, I become a reluctant lover toward Will. An obligatory lover. A tired lover. A lover with no sense of enjoyment for my husband. It's a sad and senseless place to be. But I think there is a solution, and it has to do with getting a new profession.

What if you and I decided to see *our marriages as our careers*— or in other words, what if we decided to become career wives? Now, before you close the book and write me off as archaic, consider the following: Your relationship with your husband is the one relationship meant to outlast all others. That includes your relationships with your friends, your parents and even your kids. When you stepped up to the altar and proclaimed undying love and devotion for that man, you were agreeing to an ideal that was instituted long ago. Just look at the way the Creator of marriage set things up in the first place. Genesis 2:24 tells us, "Therefore a man shall leave his father and mother, and shall cleave unto his wife: and the two shall be one flesh" (*KJV*). The idea here is that when a man and woman come together in marriage, they are to cling to each other above all others and become one. The oneness God created is designed to be the prevailing union.

But let's pull apart this verse further. There's the "leave his father and mother"—that's pretty self-explanatory (and necessary, I might add). And quite often we hear about the sexual and emotional aspects of becoming "one flesh," but have you ever stopped to consider the "cleave to his wife" part? I hadn't thought about it a lot until last summer.

I invited some newly married women to a Bible study at my house. Once a week during the month of July, we'd meet to cook dinner and talk about marriage. For the very first meeting, I decided to direct them to Genesis to discuss God as the originator of marriage. As I was reading and taking notes on the verse, I kept stumbling on the husband's need to cleave to his wife. In this section of Scripture, "cleave" is actually a passive verb that means "stick to." I think of it like Velcro: I am one piece (the "stick to" piece that's soft and fuzzy) and Will is another (the rough piece). As I kept thinking about my husband sticking to me like Velcro, I continued to try to understand what exactly God was getting at in the verse. The longer I thought about it, the more I began to see that we as women have this great capacity to be "stuck to," if you will. And in reading this verse, it became clear to me that it is actually our role to be sticky, or "cleavable." It's part of our job description as a wife. And so I started wondering what it takes for a woman to be incredibly "cleavable" to her husband . . .

How Cleavable Are You?

I asked my newly married friends this question, and we came up with some great answers. For one, a man would want a *strong* wife to cleave to. A *loving* wife. A *kind* wife. A wife that is *fun* to be around. We came up with lots of answers, and all were a little different, depending upon the husband. But the one that we didn't come up with occurred to me much later. And it is very important—it is *a wife who provides space to cleave to.* Here's what I mean. As women, we're really "sticky" people. I think a large part of that is because we are so naturally relational and, as a result, we become an invaluable person in many people's lives. We have big hearts and an unthinkable capacity to care for many different people all at the same time.

Just think about it. How many people are cleaving to you for help at this moment in time? Maybe it's your ailing mother or a friend going through a rough stretch. Perhaps it's the people you work with, always leaning on your dependability. Or maybe it's your kids—they're cleaving to you 24/7 because mothering is the ultimate "sticky" job. If you imagine your life as a strip of soft, fuzzy Velcro, with all these people and jobs hanging on to you, you can begin to see the fullness of your life.

Sacrifice always seems to imply a bitterness attached to it, but I don't feel bitter about the choices I've made. Yes, I've sacrificed a job because I've made certain family decisions, but I don't regret it.[2]

—Dana Reeve, caregiver and wife of actor Christopher Reeve, who suffered complete paralysis after a riding accident

---

But what happens when all these people and situations find a spot in your life and cleave, just hanging on for dear life? What happens to you—and what happens to your husband? Because, after all, there is only so much of you to cleave to. Sometimes, after everyone takes their spot, sticking to your life, it might leave just a little, itty-bitty spot for your husband—the one and only person on the list who is biblically commanded to cleave to you in the first place! It's as if all the soft, fuzzy spots of your life are reserved for everyone else and, inevitably, the love in your marriage relationship languishes.

When Things Get a Bit Sticky

It's a common occurrence for women to experience the "stickiness" of a busy lifestyle. So many women spend their days stuck to their kids' schedules—driving sons and daughters all over town to make sure that they're playing sports on elite teams, going to the best schools, getting top-notch music lessons. And they end up spending literally all their available time and energy raising them. Or maybe you've seen women who are committed to social activities, spending 50 hours a week working for the community good. Or possibly the women you know have a professional career and are using their intellect and business savvy to pull ahead in the work world. And don't forget those women in "sticky" situations at the local church—spending countless hours teaching Bible studies or volunteering.

While all of these are worthy endeavors—deserving of an entire lifetime of devotion—they must take second place to marriage. If we are true disciples of God's Word, we must acknowledge that our husbands come second only to a personal relationship to God. If we are staying true to the Genesis outlook, our husbands are to leave their parents and cleave to us—creating oneness. And yet, I wonder if when we're being honest, if that's the case. Could we say our husbands get the kind of quality attention and energy that everything and everyone else gets in our lives? Could we say that the men we married have a place in our lives? Do we have any room left for them to cleave—or is the rest of the world taking up all the space?

Considerations of a Career Wife

To become a career wife, we need to emulate the same kind of motivation we see in the business world. We need to muster the kind of enthusiasm for our husbands that we create for our jobs and our children.

What would it take to rethink marriage as a career? It would take a bend-over-backward devotion to the man we married. It would take considering him first before others. Proverbs 31:11 speaks of a career wife and describes her this way: "Her husband depends on her, and she never lets him down" (*CEV*). That "never letting down" energy is what many of us put into our children or jobs or volunteer work—but what about our husbands?

If you want to become a career wife, then you have to stop thinking of your husband as "just a job." Your husband is *just a job* when he becomes just one more thing on your to-do list. That *just a job* mentality will kill any excitement in your relationship. You will lose the vibrancy needed to enjoy your marriage. The attraction will fizzle and you will fall into a ho-hum existence with the man of your dreams. When we fall into that kind of trap, we no longer appreciate the gift of marriage itself. We start thinking that our love is fading and the fire has died.

But there is hope. You can start to make a career move by putting your husband first on the list. Of course it might take some ingenuity and on-the-job training, but that's what it takes to succeed in a career, right?

Consider branding yourself as a career wife. Now, I mean more than just wearing a wedding ring—though that's a great start! But how about branding yourself as a wife who will defer to her husband before others. It might be as simple as waiting to talk with him first before making commitments to others, whether at work or your kid's school or your book club. Think in terms of promoting your marriage above every other person or activity.

Another way to be a career wife is to engage in ongoing career training. Some of my most inspiring marital insight comes from perusing books about marriage. I generally try to read at least one new book on marriage each year. These valuable resources encourage me as a wife, helping me to reflect on and nourish the longest-lasting relationship of my life.

And be sure to dig into what the Bible says about marriage. Consider doing a study that concentrates on biblical marriage— you could even get a small group of friends to join you. Or attend a marriage enrichment seminar in your area.

Then think about meeting with a friend to encourage you in your marriage. I meet with a friend monthly. We go deep. We ask hard questions, and we commit to encouraging each other to love our husbands above all others.

You might also consider finding a mentor (preferably someone who has some years of experience) at your church to guide you through the heart actions necessary to becoming a career wife.

And finally, start acting like you mean it, just like you would in any other career. Get serious about making your husband the main concern of your life. Think in terms of building a portfolio of experiences with your husband. Serve him, date him, love him and pray for him. Make him an obvious priority in your life—and you will be well on your way to being a career wife. A wife who *loves* her "new career."

The Success of Stick-to-itiveness

Recently I was talking with my father-in-law about his marriage of 52 years. We were sitting in a hospital waiting room during my husband's shoulder surgery. As we were laughing and talking, I decided to ask him what it takes to stay married for over half a century. And do you know what he said? "Stick-to-itiveness." Now, I hadn't been talking about this chapter or my ideas about marriage at all. I was just genuinely curious about the longevity of his marriage to my precious mother-in-law, who 10 years ago had a horrible bout of septicemia that created serious, ongoing health issues. He asserted that it's all about making the commitment at the altar, a commitment that stands *no matter what*. Now, you must know that this is a man who has a vibrant legal career as an attorney. At one point early on in his marriage, he had the opportunity to run for governor, but he declined because he felt that he would be putting his wife and family second to his professional career. In other words, he made a decision early on to make his marriage his first priority. Isn't that interesting? His stick-to-itiveness led him to become a career husband.

Truthfully, that is a biblical mandate for marriage. That both you and your husband make a career out of your relationship, a career that exceeds the demands of another activity or job. Including a professional livelihood. Including parenting. Including all others—as long as you both shall live.

Loving Your Man

- What are the kinds of things that make "love grow cold" in your relationship with your husband?

- What unique qualities do you think make you especially cleavable to your husband? (For example: your humor, your dependability, your super-sexy, sizzling body?)

- List five people or things that really stick to you in your daily life. Now evaluate, using a scale of 1 to 5, which items or people are the stickiest.

- What would it take for you to become a career wife? How feasible is that in your life?

- While most of your time might be spent caring for children or at work, how can you still make your husband your top priority?

- List eight things you can do to become a career wife. Try enacting at least one a week for the next two months in an attempt to build some bend-over-backward devotion.

e-Group

Several years ago, if you had asked my husband where he was on my priority list, he'd have responded something like this: "I come after her job, the kids, the animals, her parents, volunteering at school, volunteering at church and her friends." Ouch! My "super-mom" mentality was costing me my relationship with my husband, Blake, and could ultimately have cost me my marriage.

Something had to give, and it couldn't be Blake anymore. For me, that meant turning my much-loved career into a part-time opportunity and eventually not working outside the home. Peeling off some "stickies" and rearranging others to make room for my husband was difficult because I had to change the way I thought about myself. It also took Blake a while to realize that I was now available to him and to trust that this newfound "clingable space" wouldn't just disappear overnight. This chapter is an affirmation that, contrary to what our culture tells women, devoting yourself to your husband is a very rewarding career move!

—Dee

Notes

1. Michael Noer, "Careers and Marriage: Don't Marry Career Women," Forbes.com. http: //www.forbes.com/business/2006/08/23/Marriage-Careers-Divorce_cx_mn _land.html (accessed May 2007).
2. "Wit and Wisdom," *The Week* (March 17, 2006), p. 35.

CHAPTER 12

The Sexiest Man Alive

What to Do When You're Attracted to the Wrong Man

Recently, my husband and about 12 other people were in Chicago at a ministry conference when the whole group decided to go out to eat after the event. While waiting for the food, a funny question was tossed out to the lively group. The question was, "If you could kiss any celebrity, who would it be?" Around the table they went, laughing and revealing secret, stalker-like crushes.

The group listened curiously as one person after another named the one celebrity they would like to kiss. One woman was so enraptured by the thought that she barely whispered her response, "Mel Gibson, on the beach, in the rain . . . wearing a kilt." By the time it was Will's turn to answer, the whole table grew quiet, waiting to hear who was the one celebrity *their pastor* would like to kiss. Will, knowing full well I would get a report of his answer before the group even returned home, chose wisely when it came time to reveal his celebrity crush. Who was the one celebrity he would most like to kiss? Angela Lansbury. The group howled at his reply, likely imagining my cute 40-something husband planting a big one on Angela's 70-something lips.

It was funny. And it was even more hilarious when the next Sunday Will stood at the pulpit to speak and found some clever, smarty-pants church member had taped a photo of Angela Lansbury to the podium. Imagine Will's surprise when he went before the church to begin his sermon and found Angela smiling up at him. They got him good!

While the question posed at dinner that night was humorously benign, there is a more serious question for married people. It's the ominous question of what to do when you are attracted to someone other than your spouse. There is real danger when you, as a married woman, find the wrong man attractive. It's dangerous because any man who distracts you from your husband has the potential to win his way into your heart and disrupt your marriage. And while it's not likely that you will be propositioned by this year's "Sexiest Man Alive," there is a good chance that there's a sexy man in the next cubicle or at your kid's soccer game who could surely have been in the running if only *People* magazine had seen him. And even though you might feel especially secure in your immunity to would-be charmers, it's always best to be aware because, honestly, there are attractive men everywhere.

Why, just yesterday, after dropping my youngest off at basketball practice, I scooted into an offbeat coffee house minutes from her school. I had just finished exercising, so I was not looking particularly glamorous. My hair was stuffed in a baseball cap, and I was wearing a T-shirt and sweats. Obviously, I wasn't thinking one bit about the fact that there are sexy men everywhere. I jumped out of the car, grabbed my laptop and headed in for a coffee drink to ward off my mid-afternoon slump. When I got to the counter, no one was there. I waited and waited and then finally called out, "Hello? Anybody here?" I felt slightly impatient, irritated that the counter help wasn't paying attention.

And then, in the very next instant, a 20-something guy came around the corner. "Sorry, I didn't realize you were here," he said, while looking me straight in the eyes, smiling mysteriously. Suddenly, I was self conscious, fumbling and uncomfortable standing there in my T-shirt and sweats.

"Um, I'll have a mocha. A small mocha," I stuttered.

"Sure thing," he replied, looking up from under his tussled, dark hair.

I watched him as he deftly concocted my mocha, wondering how in the world I went from my self-assured, 40-something persona to some shy and self-conscious, even blundering, woman. It startled me to realize that he had sidetracked me. This young guy was just plain sexy, and his presence immediately transformed me from a busy, hard-working mom into a distracted, curious *woman*.

Author Elizabeth Gilbert explains the transformation this way,

> Let's be honest, ladies. Is there anyone among us who doesn't know what manliness is? Or exactly how we feel when we meet it in person? In a Sicilian market, I once encountered a handsome butcher who exuded manliness with such force that I could barely look at him; all I could do was smile, blush, stare at my shoes, and wish he would kidnap me. He was dangerous powerful stuff.[1]

The manliness described by Gilbert is that Brad Pitt kind of appeal, and it is indeed very powerful stuff. And you've got to admit that celebrities aren't the only men capable of exuding sex appeal. (Just check out the coffee house right down the street from my daughter's school, and you'll see what I mean!)

Why All Women Are "That Kind of Girl"

Now before you write off this chapter and tell me that you simply aren't that kind of girl—I want to remind you of something. God designed men to be attractive to women and women to be attractive to men. He created the sexes to be "twitterpated" in each other's presence. And just because our culture has attempted to completely neutralize the differences doesn't mean a genderless society exists. Men and women are attracted to each other sexually. And being equal in the boardroom doesn't mean that all the sexual tension is gone. While I am grateful for all the advances for women professionally, I think the refusal to acknowledge ongoing male-female sexual tension is just plain stupid.

Most people, of course, feign ignorance concerning the matter. Yet that sexual tension is the reason it bothers you when one of your husband's coworkers is the smartest, sexiest woman you've ever seen. Ditto for your husband when it comes to the new manly coworker in your office. Your husband doesn't like it. And he shouldn't. It is reasonable and acceptable for your husband to feel protective about your marriage relationship. As a matter of fact, if Will didn't care about whether I spent time working with handsome, distracting men all day, I would worry about his feelings for me. I expect him to want me all to himself, and I wouldn't want it any other way.

Attractions are a fact of life when men and women work side by side.[2]
—Psychologist and marital researcher Shirley Glass

The goal, of course, is to be able to work well with the men in your world, whether in the boardroom or at the ball field, and not allow them to distract you from your marriage. That requires something called professionalism—not necessarily in relation to your job, but in relation to your marriage. Professionalism in your marriage is similar to professionalism at work. It's adhering to a certain standard in order to endue honor and respect. A professional person doesn't do things that create ethical issues concerning his or her job. Likewise, if you are serious about honoring your marriage, you won't exhibit behavior that creates questions about your allegiance to your spouse.

It's this simple: When you are around men other than your husband, you need to be careful about how you interact with them. Be constantly aware of the fact that you are female and they are male. And this is especially true if you realize they are attractive to you, whether physically, emotionally or spiritually. Any attraction is a warning to maintain a "professional" posture. Keep your emotions (and your hands) at a safe distance. No flirty, doe-like eyes. No gentle touches. No lingering and laughing. Everything about you must speak to the fact that you are married. From the ring on your finger to the look in your eyes. The complete package says loud and clear: "I'm happily married here." Anything else is a hazard to your marital relationship because carelessness creates entanglement with the wrong man.

Be ruthless in executing healthy boundaries. Protect your heart and thereby shield your marriage from harm. Proverbs 4:23 says it this way: "Above all else, guard your heart, for it is the wellspring of life" (NIV).

Being a Professional Wife

As a woman, I have found that guarding my heart often means watching the way I dress when I am in the company of men. Though I'm no 20-something hottie, I realize that my body is still distinctly feminine and I am still capable of catching a man's eye. And while it is flattering to be "appreciated," I have no intention of sharing my body with anyone except Will, so advertising otherwise is very unprofessional.

In addition, I am constantly mindful of the way I communicate. I really have to keep this in check because I like men. I am intrigued by their manliness. And I love the banter that is unique to male-female interaction. Yet if I am not careful, that interaction can put me in a precarious position.

Flirting is not part of an innocent friendship.[3]
—Bonnie Eaker Weil

Years ago I learned a valuable lesson about the risk of dropping my guard where verbal communication is concerned. I was rehearsing a drama sketch with a guy on our church arts team (a director was also supposed to be present to coach us, but she called and canceled because a family issue had come up and she couldn't make it). Since we were already there, we decided to go ahead with the rehearsal. We ran lines as long as we could, but because we lacked a director, we lost focus and ended up just talking. The talking led to laughing and joking and to some mild flirtation. About a half-hour later, we each headed home. Now, nothing happened between me and this guy, but what I realized while driving home is that something unprofessional *could have happened*. It scared me senseless. The minute I got home I told Will what had transpired and confessed that the whole scene had frightened me. I understood how fast and easy it would have been for me to take deadly baby steps in the wrong direction.

The Power of Two

Will and I certainly do not underestimate the danger of being attracted to the wrong person. We have seen enough marriages crash and burn to realize that no one is immune from temptation, so we created guidelines in our marriage to safeguard our relationship. One of them is that we have a practice of not meeting with members of the opposite sex without having other people around, even in our work settings. I know that might sound prudish and unrealistic in today's business environment, but it is something that we feel protects our marriage. We have both found that by eliminating the risk, it nullifies the opportunity.

Another safeguard we have in place is openly discussing the temptations that we face individually. By being open about our struggles, we diffuse the enticement (which is why when I had the unchaperoned drama rehearsal, I told Will about it). Not only does openness like this create instant accountability, but it also serves to make any temptation seem much less appealing. Of course, confession also reduces the strength of secrecy and shame. I don't want to give the enemy a stronghold in my marriage by covering up an issue instead of confessing it. First John 1:7 tells us that if we walk in the light like Jesus, we can have fellowship with one another, but if we stumble around in the darkness, we are alone. I want to have fellowship with Will. And that means Will knows about my temptations, especially the ones that could directly impact my relationship with him.

A keen sense of intimacy develops in marriage when a couple is willing to be completely honest about temptation. It's that raw honesty that is required to fortify a marriage, for a strong alliance emerges when a husband and wife have each other to strengthen their marriage against the enemy.

Honesty is the trump card for preventing affairs.[4]
—Peggy Vaughan

Run in the right direction when distracted by those manly men out there. Run to God to guard your heart, and then turn your arms to embrace the one man on Earth who deserves to receive your undivided attention—your husband.

Loving Your Man

- In the words of Elizabeth Gilbert, "Let's be honest, ladies . . ." Have you ever felt the rush of being face to face with a man who exuded extreme sex appeal? How did it make you feel?

- Why is insisting that you are above temptation particularly dangerous? Do you assume your husband is above temptation? How is the thinking that your marriage will always be safe a pitfall?

- What happens when your sin remains hidden? How does that impact your marital relationship? How does confession diffuse temptation?

- What are some "professional guidelines" you could put in place to ensure the health of your marriage?

- What will ultimately keep your marriage safe?

e-Group

I like men. I like women who like men. I am not talking about "man eaters," as in women who devour men as a hobby, but women who genuinely enjoy the company of men. When I first started reading this chapter, I read it lightheartedly, enjoying the stories of cute (read: young) coffee shop guys and mysterious Sicilian men.

But, as Susie's reflection continued, I realized that this was a very serious chapter. Although I haven't *purposely* dressed provocatively or encouraged a man's attention, I wonder if I have done these things without realizing it. This chapter made me reconsider the various aspects of my professional relationships with men and the relationships I have with the men I know from church and community activities.

And I have to admit that confessing to my husband a misplaced "attraction" is not something I had considered. Ugh, what wife wants to talk about that with her husband? But I can see how the pull and mystery is far less appealing once out in the open.

At the beginning of the chapter, I could have easily answered the "Which celebrity would you most want to kiss?" question with "George Clooney," but by the end of the chapter I didn't want to kiss anybody but my husband, Steve.

—Liz

Notes

1. Elizabeth Gilbert, "It's a Guy Thing; Manliness: What Is It? Who Has It? Does the World Need More of It—or Less?" *O Magazine,* April 1 2006, p. 228.
2. Katherine S. Peterson, "Infidelity Reaches Beyond Having Sex," *USA Today,* January 8, 2003. http://www.usatoday.com/news/nation/2003-01-08-workplace-usat_x.htm (accessed May 2007).
3. Ibid.
4. Ibid.

SECTION FOUR

Friendly Fire

Friendly fire. It's the term used by the United States to describe the distressing circumstance when military personnel are mistakenly killed or wounded by their own comrades. It happens most often when a soldier incorrectly identifies the ally as an enemy, resulting in an inadvertent attack on friendly forces by friendly forces. The military has been working hard to eliminate these horrific mistakes. As a matter of fact, many Army vehicles now have onboard computer systems that are designed to eliminate friendly fire altogether by revealing ally locations. "It tells you where you are, where your friends are and where the enemy is," said Colonel Peter Fuller.[1] So even on a dark night, the soldiers are able to identify who is friendly and who is not.

In marriage we often experience a type of friendly fire—the very things that are there to bless a marriage can sometimes tear it apart. Things like the kids. Or a house. Or money. And even extended family. Those blessings in life can become warped, and instead of supporting the marriage, they attack it. They are positioned in a place that drains the marriage instead of replenishing it.

This section will uncover the ways that the "friendlies" in our life erroneously fire on our marriage. We'll expose where "your friends are and where the enemy is" by taking a biblical look at how to handle issues that create hostility in otherwise peaceable marriages. We'll navigate issues like finances, child rearing and even getting along with the in-laws.

Note

1. Dan Ephron, "At War: The Military's Fight Against Friendly Fire," *Newsweek* (October 30, 2006), p. 8.

CHAPTER 13

Money Mayhem

When Finances Unfairly Influence Your Future

Recently we adopted a little kitten. Well . . . recently a little kitten adopted us. Two months ago, a six-month-old black stray wandered into our garage, mewing. My daughter Sara alerted me to the situation, pleading, "Mom, there's a tiny, scared kitten in our garage! Poor little thing! We need to help her."

I had a very concrete idea about how to help the poor little thing: Take her out of the garage, tightly close the door and let her find her way home. See, I am not a cat person—no wait, let me rephrase that. I *wasn't* a cat person. But the adorable nature of the kitten and my daughter's persuasive ways changed my mind. We have a cat and her name is Madeleine. I love Madeleine. She is silky and small. She is tidy and quiet. She is affectionate yet unobtrusive—the perfect cat for a person like me, who actually isn't a cat person at all.

With that said, you should know that I know nothing about cats. I grew up in a family that only had dogs. So when Madeleine arrived, I had to call "cat people" to find out things like what to feed the cat and how to care for the cat because I knew nothing about basic cat health and behavior. I, along with the rest of my family, am learning all things pertaining to cats.

In the beginning, it was delightful. Madeleine meekly eating her food. Madeleine wildly chasing the fuzzy toys. Madeleine quietly sleeping, curled up at my feet. Madeleine chattering excitedly at the birds outside our window. And there was just nothing like listening to Madeleine purr while I gently stroked her back. And then something really weird happened. Madeleine changed— she *really* changed. She went from a demure lovely feline to, for a lack of a better description, a demented little hussy. She started writhing on the floor with her eyes half closed, murmuring a sickly meow. She started howling loudly at the front door, attempting to escape whenever the door opened. And if I dared to try to pet her, her tail went straight up in the air in the most disgusting way. I wondered what in the world was happening to my little kitty, and then a hazy memory surfaced. I vaguely remembered the veterinarian mentioning something about the strange behavior of a cat in heat.

There's really no describing what was happening, but I must say it was the most dramatic, grotesque transformation I have ever seen. This kitten's capacity to go from a sweet, fantastic little pet to a freakish, uncontrolled animal overnight was mindboggling. It truly looked like she was possessed. As a matter of fact, she looked so tormented that I called the vet clinic to ask some questions because I really thought she must be in pain. I described the complete change of personality, the obvious discomfort and the unsettling behavior to the receptionist on the phone. "Should I bring her in? Is she in pain?" I asked, hopeful for help with the situation.

I was quite shocked to hear the answer: "No, she's not in pain. She's just being controlled by her hormones, and to put it bluntly, she's extremely horny."

Enough said. I thanked the woman and hung up the phone.

Are You Under the Influence?

Just to let you know, we got little Madeleine spayed and she is now the same sweet, demure kitty we met in the beginning. But I have to say that experience opened my eyes to something. And that something isn't a revelation about cats in heat and their hormones; rather, it's the startling nature of being completely overwhelmed by something. About being overwhelmed by something so big that it changes everything about who you are and how you act. *It's about being under the influence.*

While Madeleine was under the influence of her feline hormones, she had a complete personality change. And although she couldn't help herself, I thought about how we willingly place our lives under the influence of things all the time—to the point that we are controlled by them. It's just what an addiction looks like. It starts as something over which we have control, but slowly, insidiously, it turns into something we cannot control. And eventually it overtakes us. It impacts how we look and act. It rules us and influences our actions to the point that we are no longer who we want to be; rather, we have become what that thing has made of us.

Have you ever considered that there are times when you are under the influence of money? I know, I know, it sounds so ominous—"under the influence of money"—but honestly, aren't we all a little like Madeleine, wildly out of control, when it comes to the green stuff? And unfortunately, we can't blame it on our hormones. Instead, we must face up to the fact that we like money—we work hard to get it so that we can spend it. And in the process of all that getting and spending, it morphs into something that overwhelms us and ultimately manages us and messes with our marriage. That's the reason we have such difficulty discussing money rationally with our spouse.

We can tell our values by looking at our checkbook stubs.[1]
—Gloria Steinem

I believe that a preoccupation with money has overtaken many marriages to the point that couples are so influenced by finances that the marriage has taken on a whole new look—one that is often negative and strife-filled. The truth is, money is the topic couples argue about most often.

The Average Overwhelmed American Couple

If you're an average couple, you fight about money. And that's understandable, because if you're an average American family, you are $20,000 in debt. On top of that, 43 percent of households spend more than they earn every year, stifling efforts to get out of debt.[2] But even if you are one of the sensible few that aren't in debt, money creates issues. I haven't met a couple yet that can claim they never have strong disagreements about finances. And while many experts claim that couples argue over money because it represents power *in the relationship*, I would assert the main reason we fight over money is because it has power *over the relationship*.

If you make about $40,000 a year, more money won't make you happier. Comparisons, though, influence your state of mind: No matter how much or how little you make, doing better than your neighbor will make you feel better.[3]

We are a people under the influence of money because we love what money enables us to do or buy. Money is the magic carpet ride to sensory heaven, whether that is a lush trip to an enviable vacation spot or a stop at McDonald's for a Coke and fries. The experts call it "affluenza." It's defined as a painful, contagious, socially transmitted condition of overload, debt, anxiety and waste resulting from the dogged pursuit of *more*.[4] In other words, it's all about keeping up with the Joneses and ever-insistent appetites.

This likely explains why just this week people were camping out on the sidewalks of major department stores up to five days in advance to get the latest Sony PlayStation. These things are selling for around $500 to $600 apiece! New Yorker Sergio Rodriguez (who was first in line at one store) explained, "This is the best game ever. It's so worth the wait. Some people may call me crazy, but I really love to play."[5] So true: We love to play. We love to play Keeping Up with the Joneses. It's a game we love so much that we are in debt and stuffed out. And it's a game that chokes the life out of our marriages because we end up filling life with things we can't afford by buying things we don't need—and then arguing about how to manage this thing that has become bigger than the marriage itself.

Being wise is as good as being rich; in fact, it is better.
Ecclesiastes 7:11

We have friends who played the game by buying more house than their income could manage. Now he and his wife are under the influence of money to the tune of $50,000. He reports that the resulting debt is an all-consuming topic in their marriage and it's a source of great stress. It's so huge that whenever they are together, the subject comes up and creates contempt. They can't seem to get a handle on how to manage the situation and are at odds about how to fix it. For this couple, money issues have transformed the marriage relationship from a safe haven into a war zone. Money issues are simply tearing these two people apart.

Upsize the Relationship, Downsize the Stuff

A little more money might solve some immediate problems, but more money can never fix the core issue. James 4:1-2 sums up the source of the issues: "What causes quarrels and what causes fights among you? Is it not this, that your passions are at war within you? You desire and do not have, so you murder. You covet and cannot obtain, so you fight and quarrel" (*ESV*). The Bible points to our passions as the root of our arguing. We want more. Bigger houses. Newer toys. Better trips. And even if we can't afford it, we march forward and in the process enter into the battleground of conflict. When we do, we are putting our number one relationship in the most precarious position—under the influence of money. Could it be that we are "murdering" our marriages by letting money have an overwhelming upper hand in our lives? Could it be that as we bow down to the pressure to upsize, we are choosing to downsize the very thing that is the most precious to us?

Robert Arkin, PhD, of Ohio State University, reports that psychological tests repeatedly link a materialistic worldview to lower levels of life satisfaction.[6]

Will and I had our fair share of struggles living an upsize lifestyle. We went through bouts of being in control of our finances and being out of control of our finances. The roller coaster was having an effect on our relationship. Then about four years ago, we got good and tired and called in some help. We invited an expert to assess our financial history. After this man looked over our spending records, Will and I joined him for an assessment meeting. I have to say, as the primary spender in the family, I did not find the meeting pleasant. The three of us sat at our dining room table, Will and I hashing it out. We made some hard choices—together—to get back to a healthy place financially and relationally.

One of the main things we came away with was this: God has hemmed us in with a certain salary, resulting in a certain lifestyle.

Therefore, we must manage our spending appetite so that it fits within our budget and salary.

The Diet for Debt

Some of keeping that spending appetite in proper form comes from partnering with Will when it comes to bill paying. I write the bills and Will balances the checkbook. It creates accountability for both of us. We both keep an eye on where we are financially. We happen to be pretty motivated not to have another meeting with our financial guy, so this kind of accountability works well. But more important than having accountability is our continually addressing the issue of contentment. Will and I are committed, individually, to keeping a downsize mentality. Practically, this means we don't want to bite off more than our budget can handle. And honestly, the only way I have found to keep a downsize mentality in an upsize world is to earnestly pray for and seek contentment on a very deep level.

Yet true religion with contentment is itself great wealth.
After all, we didn't bring anything with us when we
came into the world, and we certainly cannot carry
anything with us when we die.
1 Timothy 6:6-7

One of the prayers I pray consistently to stave off my appetite for things and the downward cycle associated with being under the influence is Psalm 119:36-37. It says, "Give me an eagerness for your laws rather than a love for money! Turn my eyes from worthless things, and give me life through your word." I credit this verse with changing my heart and my spending habits. Every time I felt the urge to buy something that was beyond our budget, I would pray for God's help. If I was at the mall and I saw something I really wanted but didn't need or couldn't afford, I would silently utter the prayer to turn my eyes from those "worthless things" and then walk away.

After months and months of practicing this, I eventually began to realize that the promptings to buy the things I didn't need or couldn't afford were actually less frequent. Even Will noticed after a while because slowly but surely the budget was buoyed by the lack of my superfluous spending. Just because I asked, God was faithful in helping me manage my appetite for things I didn't need and couldn't afford.

Stay away from the love of money; be satisfied with what you have.
Hebrews 13:5

You see, the thing is, a working budget is great, but if discontentment is the real issue, then the budget is a demanding, frustrating taskmaster. What Will and I realized is that we needed a change deep on the inside, where our passions lie. We desperately needed God to excise the problem that was "waging war" in our hearts. Our desire to buy more and more or to keep making a constant upgrade was really an internal war we were individually struggling through. And so many of the arguments Will and I had were about managing our collective appetites— which were bigger than our salaries. We had to sit down and decide what was really important—and realistic—and work *together* at living within our means, not above it.

Wealth is like seawater; the more we drink,
the thirstier we become.
—Arthur Schopenhauer

Real Wealth

If you are arguing with your husband about debt, levels of spending or time spent working to maintain a certain lifestyle, then perhaps you should consider that your marriage is under the influence of money. And I want to add a little pressure in hopes of motivating you to think honestly about a few things. First, you should know that your marriage doesn't have to work like that. You don't have to argue and fight about money. It might take a lot of faith to imagine your marriage free from financial conflict, but it can be a reality. Second, think about downsizing your lifestyle to upsize your marriage. If you could live in a smaller house in peace with the man you married, would you do it? If you could cut out a few expenditures to have a happy family, would that motivate you? It certainly does me. There is not a house on the planet I would exchange for the blessing of a happy husband and family, because real wealth is about understanding that people are the greatest treasure.

My grandfather wrote a poem back in 1962. Whenever I read it, it reminds me that I am really the richest girl in the world.

Real Wealth

The wealth of a man seems to be measured today
By the amount of real money that he's tucked away.
It seems to me wrong that the value is there,
If we count all our blessings each day that we share.
I figure my wealth by the friends that I have,
My wife, sons and daughters, and children they have.
Their love and affection no money could buy;
You can't place a value, it's useless to try.
Our love just grows stronger; it's sweeter each day.
And I will enjoy it 'til I pass away.
So this is the wealth that I proudly still hold

And would not give it up
For a chest full of gold!

—Jay W. Gerrie

Loving Your Man

· How might your marriage be under the influence of money? If you are a dual-income family, do you feel tied to your job?

· What's at the root of your conflicts over money? Is discontentment an underlying issue?

· How would your marriage relationship look if you had no financial problems? How far is your marriage from that reality?

· What would you be willing to do without to have a peaceable marriage?

· Where is the real wealth in your marriage? In your family? How will you ensure that the reality of real wealth stays front and center in your heart and mind?

e-Group

My husband, Blake, is a wonderful provider. He works long, hard hours running his own construction company so that I can be a full-time wife and mother. We live in a beautiful home with a pool. We enjoy water skiing and hanging out at our lake cabin. We snow ski in the winter and scuba dive in the summer. Blake works hard, earns good money and enjoys spending it—and most of the time, so do I. I truly know what it means to live the good life.

But I also know the devastation of bounced checks, bank fees and large credit card balances with high interest rates. And the fun we had on our last trip doesn't come close to compensating for the awful, unrelenting feeling I so often have that the bottom is about to drop out. Blake and I just aren't usually on the same page when it comes to spending. Although I agree that we can afford to buy nice things and go fun places, I don't think we can do it at the pace that he sets. That's when the panic sets in for me, and more times than I would like to admit, that's when I start in on Blake. But the badgering just makes us both miserable and doesn't change anything for the better. Prayer, this chapter has reminded me, is what will work (it's both the easiest and the hardest thing for me to do).

So, I am going to pray instead of giving him a guilt trip. Pray instead of looking over his shoulder every time he writes a check. Pray instead of hounding him when I open the credit card bill. And pray for trust in God because I know He wants Blake and me to find real contentment in Him and not in things and places. I will pray, because God makes positive changes in people's hearts and minds—poor attitudes don't.

—Dee

Notes

1. Gloria Steinem, quoted in "Wit and Wisdom," *The Week*, March 3, 2006, p. 17.
2. Kim Kahn, "How Does Your Debt Compare?" *MSN Money*. http://moneycentral. msn.com/content/SavingandDebt/P70581.asp (accessed May 2007).
3. Kathleen McGowan, "The Pleasure Paradox," *Psychology Today*, January/February 2005. http://www.psychologytoday.com/articles/pto-20050119-000005.html (accessed May 2007).
4. "Affluenza," Wikipedia.org. http://en.wikipedia.org/wiki/Affluenza (accessed May 2007).

5. "Armed Thugs Shoot 1 Person Waiting in Wal-Mart PlayStation Line," FOX News.com, November 17, 2006. http://www.foxnews.com/story/0,2933,230182,00. html (accessed May 2007).

6. Lacey Beckmann, "Man's Best Friend?" *Psychology Today*, November/December 2002. http://www.psychologytoday.com/articles/pto-20021118-000001.html (accessed May 2007).

CHAPTER 14

Catering to the Kids

Keeping the Little Ones from Taking Too Big a Space

As I write this chapter, Christmas is just around the corner—14 days to be exact—and I haven't even started getting ready. While other people are busily checking things off their shopping lists, I am anxiously typing away in an attempt to turn in this manuscript on time. I have made a mental note to never again accept contractual deadlines that end the last week of December. It was somewhat insane of me to think that I could calmly complete a 50,000-word manuscript, purchase creative and thoughtful gifts, decorate a tree (we've had our tree up for three days, and no ornaments or lights yet!), and celebrate three family birthdays all in the same month. And it was dumb to forget to factor in that life keeps rolling with bits of the unexpected.

Like just this morning. The phone rang bright and early—it was my son. Will III is a sophomore at Baylor University, relishing life as a college student. But today he didn't sound so great. I knew something was up because he generally doesn't call at 7:30 in the morning—such *early* hours are sacred sleeping time for my 20-year-old. Today was different. He had woken up sick with chills and vomiting. As I listened to him describe his symptoms, I attempted to determine if it was the Taco Cabana run he'd made sometime after midnight or if it was the stomach flu.

Hearing his tired voice made me feel disheartened. First of all, it was his birthday. And it rattled my mothering sensibilities to think of him lying in his bed sick and shivering, alone on his twentieth birthday. And second, it really bothered me to hear how weak he sounded. It only took about two minutes of listening to his feeble voice for me to offer to drop everything I was doing and drive to Waco some two hours away. In my mind I could already see myself, standing over his bed, cool hand towel on his forehead, spooning bits of cherry Jell-O into his mouth, quietly singing happy birthday. It just tore me up thinking of him there—and me here. Forget Christmas. Forget the deadline. This is my baby boy we're talking about! It honestly didn't surprise me too much when Will III declined my offer to drive to Waco and feed him some Jell-O. Though I persisted, he politely refused. "Mom, I'll be alright. I'll call you if I need anything—really."

But something else happened a little while later that really did take me by surprise. After getting off the phone, I settled in with my laptop, determined to tackle my deadline. I was still thinking, *Will III might call back, so I should really plow through some work just in case.* I poured another cup of coffee, tucked the cordless phone by my side and then just as my fingers hit the keyboard, I heard someone coming in through the garage. I wasn't expecting anyone, so it startled me when my husband walked in. Apparently, he had a little time and decided to drop by the house after a breakfast meeting nearby. He sauntered in, coffee in hand, and I knew right away what he wanted . . . my attention.

Now that wasn't especially surprising, he does like my attention. And every once in a while, he drops by during the day unexpectedly. No, what startled me was my reaction. Immediately, I felt put-upon by my husband. Right away I thought, *What is he*

doing expecting attention from me when I have so much on my mind?!
My husband, of all people, knows how busy I am right now. He knows that
I have tons to do. He knows the pressure I am under to turn in this book
and prepare for Christmas! And just as I was thinking these thoughts,
feeling irritated and angry, I glanced down and noticed the cordless phone at my side—a reminder that I was "on call" for my
college-aged son. For me, it was one of those holy knocks on
the head. As I looked at the phone and then back up at my husband, I realized how quickly and carelessly I had put my child's
needs over those of my husband.

On-Call Mothering

The whole scene reminded me of the tension most women feel—
the tension to balance the priority of being a good mother *and* a
good wife. I don't know many mothers that don't struggle with
that pressure. Mothering creates a feeling of being constantly on
call. And it doesn't matter if the child is 2 years old or 20; the
responsibility is ever-present.

Mothering generates a sort of "drop and go" mentality. No
matter what time of day or night, no matter how important the
business, a mother will routinely drop everything to go and help
a child. From the time that first squawky cry leaves an infant's
lips at the hospital, a mother's heart is in tune with and desirous
of meeting a child's needs. It's like there is an internal pager,
much like what doctors carry, that beeps out a signal. That
parental pager beeps and a mother will dutifully respond. And
while it is a beautiful thing for a woman to give so much of herself to her child, it can become a problem when her desire to
meet her child's needs becomes so all consuming that it usurps
the marital relationship. Over time, so many women forget who
they are as wives.

*Children seem to be a growing impediment for
the happiness of marriages.*[1]

—Rutgers University's National Marriage Project
2004 Annual Report

While a woman's job is to love her husband *and* her children, problems arise when she places her children above her husband. It's easy enough to understand how that can happen. While children are growing, their needs keep changing and expanding, and it's a mother's role to change and expand right along with her children. But as a mother fulfills her role, she can easily lose focus on her marriage. Her never-ending to-do list creates an energy drain, and she fails to remember that she is a woman with other responsibilities to *another important person*. And that important person is her husband. He is the one who needs his wife's companionship. He needs his wife to be a helpmate. And he also needs his wife to be a sexual partner. The truth is, according to God's Word, it is a wife's first responsibility to love and meet the needs of her husband.

How a Wife Is Like the Church

In order to understand the biblical model for marriage, let's start with a husband's role. Ephesians 5:25-33 explains that a husband's role model is Christ Himself and a husband's job is to act toward his wife the way that Christ acts toward the Church:

> Husbands, love your wives, just as Christ loved the church and gave himself up for her to make her holy, cleansing her by the washing with water through the word, and to present her to himself as a radiant church, without stain or wrinkle or any other blemish, but holy and blameless.

In this same way, husbands ought to love their wives as their own bodies. He who loves his wife loves himself. After all, no one ever hated his own body, but he feeds and cares for it, just as Christ does the church— for we are members of his body. "For this reason a man will leave his father and mother and be united to his wife, and the two will become one flesh." This is a profound mystery—but I am talking about Christ and the church. However, each one of you also must love his wife as he loves himself, and the wife must respect her husband (*NIV*).

In reading this section of Scripture, it is evident that marriage is well defined through the metaphor of Christ and the Church. As Christ gave Himself up and died for the Church, men are asked to give themselves up and "die" for their wives. And although I don't completely understand all the implications of this Scripture passage, whenever I read it, I think to myself, *Wow, big job. Glad that's Will's responsibility, not mine.*

But then I have a responsibility, too. If Will's job as a husband is to reflect Christ, mine as a wife is to reflect the Church. So how does the Church respond to Christ? Or how *should* the Church respond to Christ? That's the best question. In the purest sense, the Church is here on Earth *to honor Christ.* Because Christ *died* for the Church, the Church in turn now *lives* for Christ. And if we apply that to marriage, it means that *we as wives should live for our husbands.*

But what does that mean practically? How do we *live* for our husbands? It's a matter of centering our lives on loving and serving them, just as the Church's whole focus is to love and serve Christ through devotion and action. It's a "Here's how I feel about you, so what can I do for you?" way of thinking. That's the approach that adequately reflects the Church's ideal response to Christ, and it's the same attitude that honors our husbands. And while that kind of devotion is one I'm hard-pressed to find in marriage, it is precisely the loving care I see good mothers extend to children every single day.

What Will I Do?

A couple of weeks ago, I met a friend for lunch. As we were talking, I noticed the conversation consistently focused on our kids. We talked about what the kids were doing and how the kids were doing. We talked about what the children's schedules looked like and how we were going to accommodate those schedules. On and on with "the kids this" and "the kids that," and finally, I asked her about her husband and how he was doing. She abruptly answered, "Oh, he's fine." And then she paused and thought for a minute, as if the question sparked a nagging irritation in the back of her mind, and added, "I don't know what I will do when the kids are gone."

While I completely understand that sentiment, it is that type of conversation that makes me realize that the problem of women prioritizing being a mother over being a wife is an epidemic. When all we are focused on doing is stuff for the kids, we are mothers at the expense of being wives, and our priorities are upside down. God never intended for a woman to sacrifice the role of wife for the role of mother. He never meant for wives to lay down the marriage relationship at the feet of child rearing.

Once my daughters began school, I was surrounded, it seemed, by women who had surrendered their better selves—and their sanity— to motherhood. Women who pulled all-nighters hand-painting paper plates for a class party. Who obsessed over the most minute details of playground politics. Who—like myself—appeared to be sleep walking through life in a state of quiet panic. Some of the mothers appeared to have lost nearly all sense of themselves as adult women.[2]

—Author Judith Warner

But what if we were able to keep the right kind of mindset about the priority that our marriages should have? What if instead of waking ever ready to serve the kids—we woke ever ready to serve our husbands? If I lived with that frame of mind, it would likely have changed the way I felt when Will walked in the door this morning unexpectedly. See, I was ready and willing to "live" my day for Will III, driving all the way to Waco and serve him—but I was not as ready and willing to "live" my day for my husband.

Biblically Based Marriage

A biblically based marriage is one in which the husband-wife relationship is the prominent relationship. That's where a healthy family starts. And as important as children are in a family, they are second to the relationship of husband and wife. It's about making sure that first things come first—and in this case, a husband comes before a child.

No doubt that sounds like a big assignment. Here you might be thinking, *If I put my marriage first, always living to serve my husband, who in the world will take care of all the needs of the children?!* Good question. But let's think logically for a minute. Husbands aren't typically terribly needy. They know how to wake up, get themselves fed and dressed. They get off to work and back without needing your help. They are really pretty independent. So I don't think that living for your husband is going to be reflected in serving him in those kinds of ways.

But how about this? Let's say it's your job to get his clothes to the dry cleaners and he notices he's low on shirts. He asks if you could please take his clothes to the cleaners. You reply, "Sure. No problem." But then in the rush of everything that's going on, you forget. So he asks again and he even offers to take in the cleaning for you. "No, no—I got it," you respond, because in the back of your mind, you know that not only is it your job, but it also means a lot to him for you to handle it. So you write it down on your agenda but still don't manage to swing by the cleaners. You do, however, manage to swing by Target and pick up a gift card for your daughter's school Christmas party—the very day she asked for it. And later that afternoon, as you hand the gift card to your daughter but have no pressed shirts ready to hand to your husband, you realize once again that you chose serving your child over serving your husband. It's unsettling, but true.

It's kind of like your heart is in the right place but your actions don't reflect it. Somehow doing all kinds of other honorable things, like taking care of the children, seems to make up for your failure to be a good wife. But honestly, neglecting to honor the one person you've pledged your life and love to because of careless or quiet disregard doesn't translate any other way. Exhausting yourself for the kids by letting them use up all your best energy, then smiling weakly at your husband, hoping he'll understand, is no way to "live" for your man.

First Things First

There is a solution. It's about making first things first. And this all starts by remembering your first love—your husband. There's an interesting verse in Revelation that addresses this situation: Jesus is speaking to the church in Ephesus. Apparently they were busy working for Christ, busy doing lots of good things. They too were struggling to do it all and keep a right focus. And while Jesus commends their hard work and perseverance, He follows by saying, "But I have this against you, that you have left your first love" (2:4, *NASB*). The church at Ephesus forgot to put first things first—Christ Himself. And so here is Jesus, seeing all the hard work and all their determination, telling them, "Just love Me again. Please put Me first."

I wonder about that. I wonder if my husband might really want to say to me, "Susie, I'm happy that you take such great care of our kids. And I'm awed by how you seamlessly coordinate everyone's schedules. I appreciate the way you have designed our beautiful home. You really astound me with the way you minister to others. But really, if you could just . . . love me again. Could you please put me first?"

Loving Your Man

- Why is it important for a marriage relationship to take priority over a parenting relationship?

- What is the ultimate goal of parenting? What is the ultimate goal of marriage? How do those different outcomes necessitate a relationship with your kids that is different from your relationship with your husband?

- A couple will parent children for only a couple of decades. Why does the parenting emphasis seem to loom over many marriage situations far longer than that time span? Is that healthy for parents or children?

- How much of an "on call" mother are you? Does that "on call" capacity cause your marriage to suffer?

- If your husband was able to be honest about his feelings regarding your devotion to the kids versus devotion to him, what do you think he would say?

e-Group

I'm looking around to try to find a huge rock to crawl under. I hope my husband doesn't ever read this chapter! I've always felt a gnawing sense that something isn't quite right with how I continually respond to Erick with, "I planned to, but didn't have time to!" I've tried to make myself feel better about it by justifying what I *have* prioritized throughout the day.

We are smack in the middle of raising three kids, ages 7 to 12. Life is busy, full, fun, challenging—and it definitely takes most of what I have to keep the house and family running smoothly (though it makes it easier to hear the part in the chapter about how husbands are really pretty independent). But Susie is right. Our husbands have to be first—and it doesn't really take a lot of time to do that.

Erick is sometimes thrown off guard if I simply laugh at his jokes (and he's pretty funny), because I'm usually preoccupied with kid stuff. Sometimes putting him first might mean a spontaneous kiss, having a conversation or taking care of some of the little things he worries about. We all know ways to make our spouses feel important or loved. Good grief, how hard is it to pick up the silly dry cleaning? I miss that one all the time because I'm always doing things that I think are more important.

It really does matter to me what we say to each other in our old age, when we look back at our lives. If I want to be secure and happy with our marriage then, I need to make it a priority now.

—Jodi

Notes
1. Sue Shellenbarger, "And Baby Makes Stress: Why Kids Are a Growing Obstacle to Marital Bliss," *The Wall Street Journal*, December 16, 2004.
2. Judith Warner, *Perfect Madness* (New York: Riverhead Books, 2005), p. 44.

CHAPTER 15

The FOO Fandango

Creating Healthy Boundaries with Your Extended Families

Ballroom dancing is big. So big in fact, that ABC's celeb-reality hit *Dancing with the Stars* pulled in over 27 million viewers for the final contest featuring three-time Super Bowl champion Emmitt Smith.[1] I am not a ballroom-dancing aficionado, but even I felt the magnetic pull to watch non-dancers like Smith samba and tango across the dance floor in garish costumes, taking down other celebrity faux-dancers vying for a slow dance in the spotlight.

But there's an even more alluring dance that continues to mesmerize me. It's a dance performed by married couples everywhere, played out in the context of extended family relationships. It's what author Martha Beck identified as the FOO (Family Of Origin) fandango.[2] The FOO fandango is determined by how a person's family of origin has impacted his or her life and continues to impact his or her current non-FOO personal relationships.

We need to understand our FOO history because it affects how we operate in our current family setting. Sometimes your FOO creates a marked desire to duplicate your parent's efforts—and sometimes it's marked by a desire to move away from your parent's efforts. Either way, it's smart to remember that our current marital interactions and parenting styles are strongly influenced by our first families.

The fact is that much of our current behavior has been influenced by an early childhood desire to fit in. As children, we attempted to fall into step with our family around us, which in essence created a behavioral dance that we brought into our adult lives. Our dance becomes second nature to us—its influence is strong, which is why, even though we marry and start our own families, that tendency to "do our dance" still resurfaces when we are in the company of our extended families. Thus, our spouse needs to learn the dance of our family of origin to know what he's up against. And so, (music please) . . . *enter the FOO fandango!*

Every marriage is a combination of two unique family cultures, and meshing those two unique cultures into a new family unit takes patience and time. While that combination is what eventually happens somewhat peaceably in the privacy of your own home with your husband, if you throw in a couple of visits to the in-laws, the pressure to dance the FOO fandango can get pretty intense. Like at a family reunion, when your spouse brings up a topic that is a no-no because it enrages Uncle Morty—and *everybody knows that*, except, of course, your husband. Or, likewise, when you are going to your in-laws for Easter and you neglect to offer to bring a side dish to help your mother-in-law, who has been slaving away Martha Stewart-style for weeks, preparing homemade everything. You didn't bring a dish—but *everyone else did*, and you leave horrified because your husband didn't give you the heads-up on his mom's expectations.

Those kinds of things happen because there are so many innate, unquestioned dance steps in the FOO that no one outside the family unit could possibly keep up with it all. Still, this puts strain on a marriage because with so many FOO moves, spouses get frustrated because they never know all the right steps. It takes years of fumbling around on the dance floor, stumbling over complex interpersonal communications (that often sound like a foreign language at first), before you and your husband finally manage to feel somewhat competent dancing with the in-laws. That's just how it works.

The FOO fandango is deeply ingrained in the psyche because of history, lots of family history, both good and bad. And while some steps are beautiful and worthy, some are better left behind. Yet for better or for worse, the steps are etched in the dancers' memories, and when they come together, a totally unique and sometimes awkward dance is set in motion. I should know—the family of my childhood has a lot of weird (we openly acknowledge our unique FOO weirdness) and wonderful dance steps. Fortunately, my husband has proved to be a more than adequate dancer of my FOO fandango. He got into the groove with relative ease, a real Emmitt Smith on the dance floor.

But I have friends—many of them—whose husbands rail against the wife's extended family relationships. Because the truth is, the FOO fandango can be an overwhelming, demanding and complex dance for any husband. And for many, it's a dance that they'd rather sit out.

What's Your FOO?

Everybody has a FOO. And if you're married, you have been partially grafted into another FOO since the day you and your husband tied the knot. The evidence of this melding of two different family cultures is most dramatically played out several years after the wedding, say when a holiday rolls around. While the holidays can be a blissful time of year, in most households they are also a stressful time, what with the shopping and party hopping and then, of course, the extra family obligations. There's just nothing like Thanksgiving or Christmas to set off the music, signaling the need to dance the FOO fandango.

Hara Estroff Marano, editor of *Psychology Today*, notes the familial tension the minute the holiday season starts.

Holidays activate everyone's longings for visibility, for recognition, for admiration, for love. At the same time, they stir old fears—of not being nurtured, of being humiliated in the eyes of others, and especially for brothers and sisters, of not being appreciated. The piling up of emotional vulnerability provides a critical mass for reaction. It's almost inevitable that the wrappings will come off family feelings.

Family holidays always ignite nostalgia about experiences in our family of origin. And just as reliably, they stir up all manner of leftover family business. Even before a holiday gets off the ground, bruised feelings and strained relations abound.

As family members pull into the driveway, they slide into old familiar roles as if they'd never left home, gotten married and started their own dynasties. In this atmosphere, nothing is natural; every act, every gesture and word is emotionally charged. Arriving and saying hello, only to find that your big sister or brother is—or isn't—there before you, can set off feelings of being slighted. As the family sits down to dinner, the stories that are told don't just stand or fall on their own merit. They resonate with who has the voice that's heard, and who spoke last time. Just whose version of that Hawaii vacation 20 years ago dominates the conversation—once again?[3]

It's that underlying history of a family that creates the music for the dance. And even though the dance is familiar, it can be achingly painful for the entire family. But that doesn't stop the dance because there's a magnetic draw to move, like it or not. And on top of that, discontinuing the dance is like dissing the family—so we dance.

But if you are an in-law, figuring out the unique beat of the FOO fandango can be challenging and somewhat maddening. You're rushing around, but all the while you're wondering, *What just happened here? That was weird.* But you're smiling just the same on the outside. It feels clumsy dancing around old relationships as new ones form. And it takes some time for everybody in the family to get used to their new in-laws (of course, the reverse is true, too).

When our relatives are at home, we have to think of all their good points or it would be impossible to endure them.
—George Bernard Shaw

But what do you do if your FOO is complicating your marriage? What if they are inadvertently (or purposefully) destabilizing your marriage? Whether it's outright dislike of your spouse, manipulative and underhanded slights, or just ongoing relational turmoil, how do you ensure the FOO doesn't disrupt your marriage for the long haul?

No Stepping on the Toes

While the Bible is clear about respecting and honoring parents (outlined in the fifth commandment), the Bible is equally clear about boundaries for the marriage relationship. In Genesis 2, the instructions for a man to *leave his father and mother and cleave to his wife* clearly indicate that the newly formed marriage is to have preeminence over any other family relationships. If there are still abiding loyalties to the FOO that supersede the marital relationship, trouble is ahead—and I really think this is where most difficulties start. If there is great disdain between your FOO and your husband, I urge you to examine whether your husband feels honored and respected by you *before* your parents. If a man feels threatened by his wife's family ties, it makes sense that he has difficulty getting along with the in-laws.

When there are blurred boundaries of allegiance in a family, people get tromped on—and most often it's the husband. As wives, it's our responsibility to honor our husbands by looking to them for leadership—which means it's time to let Mom and Dad go. It's time to release them from their parenting privileges and move on with life, though that is sometimes easier said than done. When a woman gets married, she moves from leaning and relying on Dad and Mom to leaning and relying on her husband—come what may. If she is unable to disentangle herself from the FOO, her marriage is in a precarious position.

I can easily step on Will's toes if I'm not careful, because I grew up with the benefit of a great dad. He was (and is) a real encourager to me. There isn't a time when I see him that he doesn't tell me how much he loves me. He always tells me he is proud of me, and he still acts very fatherly, which is a tremendous blessing. But just to illustrate how crossing the line between honoring your parents and putting them before your husband looks—let me create a scenario.

Let's just say Will and I got in a horrible fight. And let's say I was so upset I called my parents, crying because I just didn't know where to turn. At that point, it might be easy for me to promote my dad to a place above Will, simply because I turned to my dad for support instead of working it out with Will. Yet that would be setting my dad up to act like a protective papa bear, as I allow him to usurp Will as my leader. I would be calling on my dad to protect me from Will, which is not healthy at all. Will would be in a no-win situation because we had a fight. And the same would be true if Will phoned his parents, incensed over something I had done. He would be pitting his family against me because of a heated moment. As the boundaries blur, the relationships move into the Dysfunctional Zone, which is a scary place for everyone.

Watch Out for the Fandango of Dysfunction

When you grow up in a family, everything is "normal" from your insider perspective. But every family has developed quirky little coping mechanisms that are somewhat dysfunctional. "Dysfunction" is just a fancy word for describing what it looks like to be outside of what God says is healthy. In many small ways, we're all dysfunctional.

But the real problems crop up when the entire family is forced to comply with the behavior of the *least* healthy person in the family. And until you are able to honestly assess your FOO's health, you are in a vulnerable place with your spouse. Because if your spouse points out the obvious ("Honey, your mom is super controlling with little Junior"), and you get mad because you just don't see it ("How dare you accuse my mom of being too controlling! She's just helping me out because you are always busy!"), then your family—your mom in particular—has the ability to step between you and your husband.

Dysfunctional relationships are rigid. Each person plays one role, and any attempt to behave differently is met by indignation or even aggression.[4]

To have a healthy marriage, you must bravely look your FOO in the face and biblically assess what is normal and what is abnormal, and what is worthy of bringing into your own family and what isn't. Then you just have to step back emotionally and allow your marriage to take first priority. This is the only way to ensure that your marriage doesn't get sucked into being a cog on the wheel of a frightening FOO fatality.

The Dirty Little Dance of Bitterness

There is another variation of the dance of dysfunction. It's the dirty little dance of bitterness, and quite often, we as the children of the FOO are the ones dancing to that tune.

There is not a parent alive that has done everything right. Parents mess up and contribute to problems in every family. No doubt you remember things your parents did when you were growing up that created serious chaos for you and your siblings. Maybe it was a divorce. Or a raging temper. Or an absence of parental authority. Maybe they didn't provide for the family financially. Or perhaps they were so busy meeting their own needs that parenting wasn't a priority. There are a million little ways that parents miss the mark. These missteps create dissonance within children that, if not reconciled, can carry over into adulthood. As a matter of fact, there are many adult children who no longer enjoy being around their parents. Some adult children would prefer to never see anyone in their FOO again—ever.

When this is the reality in your life, it's the perfect set-up for the dirty little dance of bitterness. Bitterness is nothing more than an ongoing lack of forgiveness. It's nursing a hurt when it's time to lay down the pain—and the blame. The serious problem with continuing this dirty little dance is that there is no way to protect your marriage from being infected in the process. If you are affected by bitterness, so are those closest to you.

Bitterness is like cancer. It feeds upon the host.
—Maya Angelou

I have a friend whose dad had an affair when she was a child. He was selfish and secretive. He was unfaithful to his wife and children. And when he left his family for the other woman, he ravaged relationships in the process. Thirty years ago, he defied the very people he should have held dear. My friend no longer speaks to her father, but it's something she talks with her husband about regularly. It's something that lurks in her mind, popping up at the strangest of times and something she seeks to manage but is not free from. The hurt still remains.

I have another friend whose parents divorced, and she's in a situation that is particularly painful: Her mother won't talk to her if she talks to her dad. This young woman recently had a baby, and her mother has yet to acknowledge her first grandchild. The animosity is so great that this new grandmother has lost sight of what is, in reality, one of the greatest blessings of her life. My friend and her husband are caught, continually assessing every action in an effort to manage the feuding parents. And my friend finds herself struggling with bitterness toward her mother. It's a continual effort for her to forgive her mother because her mother is re-inserting poison from a past hurt into her life. It's devastating—and it's draining the life from my friend and her young marriage.

That is the result of the dance of bitterness. It creeps into our lives and steals joy and energy from our most important human relationship of all.

See to it that no one misses the grace of God and that no bitter root grows up to cause trouble and defile many.
Hebrews 12:15, NIV

If you spend significant amounts of time managing old hurts from your family of origin, I can promise you that it's affecting your marriage. Those nights you spend talking about how your "dad did this" or your "mom does that" are signals that you are FOO fandango-ing the dirty little dance of bitterness. That dance is the most exhausting, confusing, dead-end dance around. And it's a dance that will monopolize a marriage—if you let it.

You Gotta Dance with the One Who *Bought* You

If you're following what I'm saying, even if it's making you sick to your stomach, then you understand the biblical need to discontinue the dirty little dance of bitterness. We aren't free to listen to the beat of our own drum. Instead, we are compelled to get in rhythm with God's Spirit. Ephesians 4:30-32 says:

> And do not bring sorrow to God's Holy Spirit by the way you live. Remember, he is the one who has identified you as his own, guaranteeing that you will be saved on the day of redemption. Get rid of all bitterness, rage, anger, harsh words, and slander, as well as all types of malicious behavior. Instead, be kind to each other, tenderhearted, forgiving one another, just as God through Christ has forgiven you.

God is very clear about His intentions. We are to dance with Him—the One who *bought* us. And the truth is, this is the only dance with steps more memorable and more compelling than the FOO fandango.

Following God's guidelines for relational living (even with the in-laws) is the only way to ensure that you and your husband stay center stage. Drawing healthy boundaries and refusing bitterness is the surefire way to really score on the familial dance floor. It's also the only way to truly honor your parents—and your in-laws. When your marriage manages to fandango with God's rules above all, then that will be the dance that everyone can understand—and appreciate.

Loving Your Man

- In what ways is your family of origin healthy or unhealthy according to biblical standards?

- On a scale of 1 to 10, rate your FOO and your husband's FOO when it comes to involvement in your marriage/ family, with 1 being uninvolved and 10 being very involved. Is there an imbalance? Why? How does the participation of each FOO affect your marriage?

- Every family has dysfunction, but in some cases, a FOO loyalty is causing the dysfunction. How does that impact your marriage?

- At this point in your life, what does honoring your parents look like? How about honoring your in-laws? Should you be doing more or less to honor them?

- Desmond Tutu has been quoted as saying, "You don't choose your family. They are God's gift to you, as you are to them." How has your family of origin been a gift to you? How has your husband's family of origin been a gift to him? How are you and your husband a gift to your respective families of origin?

e-Group

Oh, my—this chapter hit close to home. I read it just after spending a hectic Thanksgiving with my new husband and my "unique" FOO. While my husband loves my family, he too is learning our

FOO dance. Suffice it to say, by the end of the long Thanksgiving weekend, he had had enough! He retreated to our bedroom, leaving me to finish the "entertaining" of family and friends. I was miffed! I knew he was tired, but what about me? At the end of the night, I stormed into the bedroom, made it clear I was angry, slept as far away from him as I could and actually jerked my foot away when it accidentally touched his!

It is a moment that we now laugh about. But after the family left, and as we faced a rapidly approaching Christmas holiday with his family, we had an honest discussion about how we can better "dance" that FOO fandango with each other's families. I think it was a discussion that we both needed. We talked about how, especially during the holidays, we need to also take time for ourselves so that our relationship doesn't feel pushed aside in all the mad FOO dancing we're doing. We talked about the importance of honoring both of our families. And we talked about learning to honor one another and our marriage before we honor our respective families. It was a discussion that reminded me that I am in this *together* with my husband. We are partners. It also reminded me that we are partnering with Jesus, and that with His guidance we can make our own family, as well as our FOOs, stronger.

—Julie

Notes

1. "'Dancing with the Stars' Finale Scores Big Ratings," FOX News.com, November 22, 2006. http://www.foxnews.com/story/0,2933,231367,00.html (accessed May 2007).
2. Martha Beck, "Debunking Five Holiday Myths," *O Magazine*, August 2006, p. 48.
3. Hara Estroff Marano, "Surviving Holiday Hell," *Psychology Today Magazine*, Nov./Dec. 1998. http://www.psychologytoday.com/rss/pto-19981101-000024.html (accessed May 2007).
4. Beck, "Debunking Five Holiday Myths," p. 50.

Chapter 16

Happy Anniversary

Making Marriage Last for a Lifetime

There's a stranger sleeping in my bed—or at least that's what I seem to think every so often at two o'clock in the morning. In the past decade I have exhibited symptoms of a sleep disorder called night terrors. While for many people this disorder is drastic and frightening, mine is fairly mild. It always manifests itself in the same way and always seems to surface when I am overloaded by life. I fall right asleep with Will at my side and within a couple of hours, I sit up in bed abruptly, look in terror at the lumpy form next to me and ask breathlessly, "Who are you?!"

Now at first, this situation was pretty confusing—especially for my husband. He certainly didn't know what to think. Startled from sleep, he would hear me frantically calling out and then grab my arm saying, "Susie! What's wrong?! What is it?!" Well, that reaction didn't help me at all. Since I was not fully awake, it actually made things worse and I would jerk away from him and continue asking, "Who are you?! *Who are you?!*"

After a couple of these bizarre occurrences, my weary, worn husband tried sarcasm when I awoke distressed and confused. In answer to my question, he would tartly respond, "Who do you *think* I am?" and wait for my response. No comfort for me there at all, and he got more of the same: "Who are you?! *Who are you?!*"

Then one night when he was particularly annoyed by my waking him, he responded to my nighttime question with, "Well, this is Lyle Lovett." (Will has an attitude about Lyle, claiming I have a "strange artist fixation" for the man because I simply *adore* his music and humor.) Now again, this was a bad idea on Will's part because even though I love Lyle Lovett and his music during the day, at night, in the middle of my terror, I was shocked and frantic at my husband's smarty response.

Over the years Will has become more forgiving about being awakened by his disoriented wife, and he has learned that the best response to the sleep-disorder question is always a soft, reassuring, "Susie, I'm your husband." And with that, I settle back into bed and go right to sleep.

A Little Living Nightmare

That whole silly situation reminds me of something: I'm a mess. A real mess. And just about the time I start to feel a little dignified or a smidge superior, I am likely to wake up my husband of 20-plus years, screaming in the middle of the night, terrified in my very own bed. And it makes me wonder to myself, *Just who is driving whom crazy?*

The other morning I overheard Will telling our daughter Emily about one of my startling nighttime awakenings. She laughed as he explained the scenario and then he finished by saying, "She's my little living nightmare!" It was really funny because he was actually quite tender while calling me his "little living nightmare," but it did make me think about how it must be to live with me. Because honestly, it's not just my weird nighttime habits that are bothersome to live with—it's also my daily blunders. There are times when I am unbearably rude toward my husband or unflinchingly selfish. There are numerous times daily that I take him for granted.

The truth is, I'm a mess. I know that I fall far short of the magnificent standard God has set for me. And that is true whether it's the standard of being a loving wife or a loving person in general. I know that I'm nowhere near deserving of all that God has gifted me with—be it His Son, Jesus Christ, who died on behalf of my sins, or my husband, who loves me in and through the marriage commitment he made to me years ago. When I compare how I love others to what God has said regarding love and marriage and the right way to treat people, I know that I'm a mess. And then when I realize that God and Will keep loving me through it all, I feel small and weak and completely grateful.

Writing this book has caused me to reflect on God's ideas about love—specifically unconditional love. Because being married and staying committed in a covenant relationship means you have someone who loves you no matter how weird or wonderful you are—it's about your husband being there, come what may. Unconditional love has given me the opportunity to be wholly real and wholly loved. There's just so much grace in that.

And honestly, it's then that I pray for *more grace* in my marriage because I know that's the only way Will and I will be capable of loving each other the way God intends for us to love. It's the unselfish love mentioned in 1 Corinthians 13:4-7:

> Love is patient and kind. Love is not jealous or boastful or proud or rude. Love does not demand its own way. Love is not irritable, and it keeps no record of when it has been wronged. It is never glad about injustice but rejoices whenever the truth wins out. Love never gives up, never loses faith, is always hopeful, and endures through every circumstance.

It's the love that is patient and kind and forgiving that never gives up. And that's the love that breeds hope—the hope it takes for any married couple to weather the years with a commitment that "endures through every circumstance."

A Faith-Filled Marriage

My parents have weathered the circumstances. As a matter of fact, we are celebrating their fiftieth wedding anniversary a week from today. My whole family is getting together to throw a dinner party at a nearby club to commemorate the big day. I can already imagine the night. There will be a delicious dinner of tenderloin, asparagus, salad and garlic mashed potatoes. The meal will be served on a table tastefully decorated with white tulips, candles and photographs of my parents with their children and grandchildren. My son will play his guitar so the younger grandkids can sing a few of my parent's favorite songs. And finally, during dessert and coffee, we will all take turns gifting my parents with words of appreciation and love.

I have been thinking a lot about what to say to my parents. I know that I'll thank them for staying married for so long. And no doubt, as hard as I'll try not to, I'll cry. I'll cry because I love them and because it's such an accomplishment to stay married that long. I'll cry because they are modeling for me and my children what it looks like to love and live together in marriage for 50 years. I can already see the whole evening in my mind's eye and, though it has yet to happen, I know it will be a meaningful evening for both my parents and our family.

In much the same way I see that evening and know it will come to pass, I can also see and know that Will and I will celebrate 50 years of marriage. Even though as of this writing, we have yet to celebrate half the years of matrimony my parents have celebrated, I have a deeply rooted belief that God will enrich and sustain our marriage. I know He will tenaciously mold us into excellent, unconditional lovers for each other.

And though today might look like any other day at the Davises from the outside in, God is at work this very minute changing us and making us sweeter for each other.

We'll make that golden anniversary with children and grandchildren at our sides. Delicious dinner and music. And with happy hearts we will celebrate the ways God formed us into who we needed to be for one another. I welcome what I'll become for Will, and what he will be for me. And I thank God in advance for all the beauty and also the inevitable hardship, knowing that He alone can make our marriage into something supremely pleasing. I smile at the future, seeing my husband by my side.

This really isn't mumbo-jumbo positive thinking. It's actually a biblical concept called *faith*. Hebrews 11:1 tells us that faith is the confidence that what we hope for will actually happen—through faith we have assurance about things we cannot see. We all need that kind of assurance for marriage because staying married for a lifetime requires that kind of tenacious faith, especially in times like these.

When statistics tell us that more than 50 percent of all marriages end in divorce, faith is believing that your marriage will not be one of those fatalities. Faith is accepting the fact that God wants your marriage to succeed even more than you do. And it's about believing that, right now, He is molding and holding the two of you together.

'Tis Grace Hath Brought Us Safe This Far . . .

Staying married for a lifetime requires a belief in what *God* can accomplish, not what *you* can accomplish. It's about having holy confidence. Though there are all sorts of actions and attitudes you can adopt to help your marriage succeed, ultimately, it all gets right back to grace.

What kind of God-sized dreams will you dare to dream for your marriage? Will you reach out for more than you can imagine—more than you ever hoped for? How about asking Him for decades and decades of "Happy Anniversary"? Because it really is His grace that has brought you this far, and it is His grace that will bring you home. The grace to love, the grace to believe—and the grace to make marriage last for a lifetime with the man of your dreams.

More Books That Offer
Big Help for Relationships

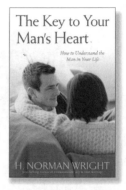

**Moments Together
for Couples**
The classic best-seller with
devotions for drawing near to
God and one another.
Dennis and Barbara Rainey
Hardcover • 384 pages
ISBN 08307.17544

**Communication: Key to
Your Marriage**
A Practical Guide to Creating a
Happy, Fulfilling Relationship
H. Norman Wright
ISBN 08307.25334

**The Key to Your
Man's Heart**
How to Understand
the Man in Your Life
H. Norman Wright
ISBN 08307.33345

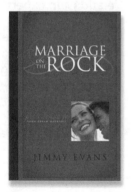

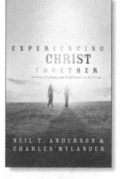

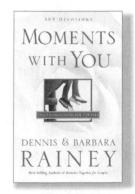

Marriage on the Rock
God's design for
your dream marriage
Jimmy Evans
ISBN 08307.42913

**Experiencing Christ
Together**
Finding Freedom and Fulfillment
in Marriage
Neil T. Anderson and
Charles Mylander
ISBN 978.08307.42882

**Moments with You:
365 All-New Devotions
for Couples**
A 365-Day Devotional
Dennis and *Barbara Rainey*
ISBN 08307.43847

Regal
God's Word for Your World™
www.regalbooks.com